HALL PASS
a play by
David Overton

LICENSING & PRODUCTION INQUIRIES
Uproar Theatrics, LLC.
hello@uproartheatrics.com I www.UproarTheatrics.com

HALL PASS

Cast of Characters:

MAKAYLA: Female. 12th grade. Socially polished. Mature.

SOPHIA: Female. 12th grade. Matter-of-fact.

SAGE: Female. 12th grade. Observant. Dry humor. Often smartest one in the room.

ILAN: Female. 11th grade. Thoughtful. Artistic. Strong personality.

BRENNA: Female. 11th grade. Competitive. Slightly sharp. Social climber.

TESS: Female. 10th grade. Young energy. Wants to be included. Learns fast.

MIA: Female. 10th grade. Quiet. Sensitive. Internalizes everything.

GABRIELA: Female. 10th grade. Comfortable in her own skin. Joyful.

FIONA: Female. 10th grade. Insightful. Realistic.

HAZELL: Female. Young 10th grade. Quiet. Wise beyond her years. Recently transferred.

NICK: Male. 11th or 12th grade. Lacrosse team captain. Charismatic. Usually confident.

EMERSON: Male. 11th or 12th grade. Logical. Tries to fix things. Avoids emotional mess.

ALEX: Male. 11th or 12th grade. Follower. Nervous. Still forming his moral compass.

MS. DESANTIS: Female. 30s to 50s. Guidance counselor. Warm, compassionate, listener.

VOICE of PRINCIPAL WALTERS (performed by the actress who plays DESANTIS)

RECORDED VOICEOVER: an adult should record this.

Props:

1. Cell phones for all

2. Purses for most

3. Backpacks for some

4. Hall passes

Playwright's Note:

HALL PASS explores a moment that has become increasingly familiar in the lives of young people: when a private moment becomes public in an instant. The play is less interested in the specifics of an image than in the ripple effects that follow; how stories form, how rumors spread, and how quickly a person can become defined by a single moment seen out of context.

The main characters in this play are teenagers navigating friendship, reputation, loyalty, and responsibility in a world where phones and social media make every mistake feel permanent. While the circumstances are contemporary, the emotional landscape is timeless: the desire to belong, the fear of being judged, and the challenge of standing by one another when it matters most.

This play should be approached with honesty, empathy, and respect for the complexity of the students portrayed. The goal is not to assign blame or offer simple answers, but to create space for conversation – about accountability, compassion, and the power each person holds in shaping the stories we tell about others.

Additional Notes:

1. Add music appropriately.

2. Don't try to make sense of the timing of the bells throughout the play; time is compressed/altered.

3. That the entire play takes place in the girls' bathroom creates the challenge of how to activate the scene – but that's exactly what performers must do. Find business that your character might do – looking in mirror, checking makeup, hair, the fit of clothing, moving to others, checking phone, wiping something off your cheek with a paper towel, making contact with the other characters; find something to do.

4. Certain scenes include phone notification buzzes from the respective characters' devices.

These should be low and distinct – audible to the audience without being jarring. They may be used alone or paired with a subtle notification tone.

5. "Oh my gah" replaces "oh my god" throughout the script as a deliberate stylistic choice, maintaining the natural tone of speech while avoiding potential concerns around language sensitivity. Additionally, the phrase operates as a verbal tic, akin to the frequent use of "like" in teenage speech, and should be understood as part of the character's rhythm and expressive habits. The pronunciation of that phrase should sound organic/natural.

6. In a high school setting, the role of Ms. DeSantis is intended as an opportunity for an adult faculty, administrator, or guidance counselor to participate in a very real, meaningful way.

Playwright's Reflection:

As the playwright of HALL PASS, I want to acknowledge that this is a story centered on the experiences of teenage girls, and as a man, I cannot claim to fully know that experience from the inside. I have approached that distance with humility, guided by the women in my life; most especially my three daughters, whose navigation of the complex and often unforgiving terrain of adolescence has deeply informed my perspective, and my wife, whose insight, empathy, and honesty have continually challenged me to listen more carefully and see more clearly. Through them, I have come to better understand the pressures, scrutiny, and resilience that shape young women's lives, as well as the persistent imbalance in expectations placed on girls versus boys.

This play is, at its core, an attempt to listen and to honor the complexity, strength, vulnerability, and humanity of young women. With deep respect and gratitude, I dedicate it to my daughters, my wife, and to all women whose stories deserve to be heard and treated with care.

HALL PASS

SETTING: Both Acts take place inside the girls' bathroom. There is a long, low counter with sinks at center (at least 4) so that actors will face the audience. The sinks have knobs and a spout – no running water but there should be water pre-set in the sink. A paper towel dispenser is attached to the stage right edge of the counter. A long mirror (imaginary) spans the length of the counter. Similarly, there is a tall, horizontal mirror on stage right of the counter. On stage left are four stalls with doors that do not reach the floor (the bottoms of toilets should be visible). The four stalls should have toilet paper rolls on a dispenser. Off-center and behind the counter is the door to the bathroom. Upstage of the bathroom is the hallway area with signs that read "KINDNESS STARTS WITH YOU" and "HAPPY HOLIDAYS."

In all the scenes, actors need to find 'business' appropriate to what they would do if they were in a public school bathroom: makeup, primping, poking, looking, assessing, fixing, smoothing, etc.

ACT I

SCENE 1

At lights up, SOPHIA and SAGE are already in the bathroom. SOPHIA stands at the counter mirror, doing something tiny and precise – mascara, concealer, lip gloss, checking her hair from different angles. Standing beside SOPHIA is SAGE, washing her hands like she is not in a hurry. SAGE's calm is real, but it is also a choice. Their phones are handy.

Bell rings.

                    SOPHIA

I hate this lighting.

                     SAGE

It's a bathroom.

                    SOPHIA

Exactly.

                     SAGE

The fluorescent lights are not plotting against you, Soph.

                    SOPHIA

They are if you have pores.

                     SAGE

Everybody has pores.

                    SOPHIA

Not the people on my "For You" page.

                     SAGE

They have pores. They just also have ring lights and free
time. They are 'without want.'

          *SOPHIA leans closer to the mirror, pulling her cheek
          back like she's inspecting a painting for cracks.*

                    SOPHIA

They may be without want, but I'll tell ya what I want...
(doesn't finish her thought). If I get one more random stress
pimple before break, I'm gonna start a petition.

                     SAGE

A petition?

SOPHIA
To the school. Like, "Dear Principal Walters. This is hostile."

SAGE
Oh my gah. Principal Walters is hostile.

SOPHIA
Exactly. She'll respect it.

HAZELL
(walks in quickly, goes into stall) Sorry.

SAGE
(quietly) Who's that?

> *SOPHIA shrugs. SAGE dries her hands. SOPHIA
> checks her phone; trying to look casual.*

SAGE
You're waiting.

SOPHIA
I'm not waiting.

SAGE
You are literally standing in a bathroom during lunch to
refresh your phone.

SOPHIA
I came in here because I literally had something in my eye.

SAGE
We've been in here the whole lunch.

SOPHIA
It was a big thing.

                    SAGE
Was it a text message shaped thing?

                    SOPHIA
Sage.

                    SAGE
Soph.

            *They stare at each other in the mirror. SOPHIA
            breaks first – she smiles, annoyed at herself.*

                    HAZELL
(coming out of stall) Sorry. *(exits)*

                    SAGE
Eww.

                    SOPHIA
What?

                    SAGE
She didn't wash her hands.

                    SOPHIA
So? She didn't pee her hands. *(checks her phone)* He opened
it.

                    SAGE
Who?

                    SOPHIA
And… nothing.

                    SAGE
Maybe he's eating.

                              SOPHIA

He's not eating. He doesn't eat lunch. He drinks those neon
sports drinks like he's being sponsored, or something.

                               SAGE

Maybe he's – I don't know – living his life.

                              SOPHIA

That's rude.

          SOPHIA caps her lip gloss with unnecessary force.

                               SAGE

Who are we discussing?

                              SOPHIA

We're not discussing anyone.

                               SAGE

Okay. Emerson.

                              SOPHIA

I didn't say Emerson.

                               SAGE

Girl, you didn't have to. Your whole face literally says
Emerson.

                              SOPHIA

My face does not 'say' people's names.

                               SAGE

Girl, it does. Your face is very communicative. If your face
had a GPA, it would be higher than mine.

                           SOPHIA
Stop.

                            SAGE
I'm just saying, if Emerson is ignoring you, it's not because
of you.

                           SOPHIA
That's the nicest way anyone has ever said, "he's a boy."

                            SAGE
Thank you. I'm very good at translating. *(beat)* Él es un
chico.

             *SOPHIA checks her hair again, but this time it's
             clearly not about hair.*

                           SOPHIA
It's just – you know when you can feel that something is…
shifting?

                            SAGE
Girl, the toilets are right over there.

                           SOPHIA
No, I'm serious! There's shifting going on.

                            SAGE
All right, shifting… like the Earth's crust, or…?

                           SOPHIA
Like people. Like – the air.

                            SAGE
The air in this bathroom is mostly hand-soap and girl-angst.
And maybe somebody ate something bad.

SOPHIA

Sage.

SAGE

Okay. Yes, whatever. It's shifting. It's December. Everyone's losing their minds. We have midterms and Mr. Halpern is acting like the Government midterm is the bar exam. When even is that?

SOPHIA

Friday.

SAGE

Friday, yes. And Coach Daniels keeps giving speeches about "integrity" like he's running for office.

SOPHIA

That speech was so long.

SAGE

Longer than the actual Constitution.

SOPHIA

He literally said, "Who are you when no one is watching?"

SAGE

And everyone was watching him say it.

SOPHIA

It's like, pick a lane.

They share a quick laugh. It keeps things light.

Bell rings.

SOPHIA

Is that our bell?

SAGE

End of first lunch, I think.

SCENE 2

> *The bathroom door swings open. TESS rushes in, FIONA right behind her. TESS is mid-rant, slightly out of breath.*

TESS

I'm telling you, if she says "annotate" one more time, I'm going to annotate myself out of existence.

FIONA

You can't annotate yourself.

TESS

Watch me. I'll put a little asterisk next to my name and then at the bottom it'll say, "no longer participating."

FIONA

If only.

TESS

(to SAGE or SOPHIA) Oh, hi.

SOPHIA

Hi.

FIONA

Oh, hi Sage!

SAGE

Hi, Fiona. How's Rowan doing? Is he behaving?

FIONA

He's fine but his accent is terrible. I mean, would it kill him to try to approximate a French accent since it's French class?

SAGE

Yeah, his French sucks. He's a good little brother but he doesn't take his meds.

FIONA

No offense, but it kinda shows.

SAGE

I mostly just can't believe he's taking French instead of Spanish.

FIONA

Then he'd just have a bad Spanish accent.

SOPHIA

Sage, come with me to get some water.

SAGE

Bye.

FIONA AND TESS

Bye!

SAGE and SOPHIA exit.

FIONA and TESS move to the mirror, inspecting.

TESS

Does this look like I tried too hard?

FIONA

Honestly? Yah.

                          TESS

Okay, but like… in a cute way or in a, like, "she woke up at
five a.m." way?

                          FIONA

In a "you definitely had time to reconsider and didn't" way.

                          TESS

(considers, nods) Okay. I can live with that. *(grabs FIONA'S
arm)* Wait. Important. Stop.

                          FIONA

What?

                          TESS

You cannot do that again.

                          FIONA

Do what?

                          TESS

The eye contact thing.

                          FIONA

What eye contact thing?

                          TESS

With that guy, Will. In the hallway. You made eye contact
with him for, like, seven full seconds.

                          FIONA

I was just looking at him.

                          TESS

No, no. That was sustained.

FIONA

Oh, and is "sustained" a level of looking?

TESS

It is. There's "glance," there's "look," and then there's…
whatever that was. That was dangerous.

FIONA

(genuinely confused) How was me looking at Will
dangerous?

TESS

They imprint.

FIONA

(blinks) …what?

TESS

They imprint.

FIONA

That's not a thing.

TESS

It is a thing! We literally learned about it in Psych class.

FIONA

Oh, in Psych, they said that boys imprint on girls who make
eye contact?

TESS

Yeah, I mean imprinting like, with animals. Ducks. Puppies.
You know how they see the first thing and then they're like,
"that's my mom now"?

FIONA

Yes, I'm familiar with ducks and puppies.

TESS

Okay, so it's that!

FIONA

That is not that.

TESS

It is! It's the same principle! You make eye contact for too long, and their brain goes, "Oh. This is my person now."

FIONA

That is not how brains work.

TESS

It is how their brains work.

FIONA

Their brains?

TESS

Boys.

FIONA

Boys are not the same as ducks or puppies.

TESS

Emotionally? That's kinda debatable, Fiona.

FIONA tries not to laugh.

FIONA

Gimme a break, I looked at him for, like, a normal amount of time.

TESS

No. It crossed over. I saw it happen.

FIONA
What does "crossed over" even mean?

TESS
There's a point where it goes from "oh hi" to "oh no."

FIONA
Oh no what?

TESS
Oh no, now he thinks you're his.

FIONA
I am not anyone's!

TESS
I know that! You know that! He does not know that! He thinks you're, like, the first warm thing he saw after hatching.

FIONA
I'm pretty sure boys don't hatch.

TESS
You don't know that.

   Beat. FIONA stares at her.

FIONA
Girl, you are insane.

TESS
Girl, I am informed.

FIONA
You are misapplying psychology.

                                TESS
Okay, but explain why he turned around?

                               FIONA
Because people turn around!

                                TESS
No. He turned around again.

                               FIONA
That doesn't mean anything!

                                TESS
It means he's imprinted. Congratulations, Fiona, you now
have a puppy!

                               FIONA
I do not have a puppy!

                                TESS
You do! It's metaphorical. But still. You have to take care of
it, you know. Like, feed it.

                               FIONA
I'm not feeding a boy.

                                TESS
Not literally. Just, like, emotionally. You have to be careful
now.

                               FIONA
Careful of what?

                                TESS
If you ignore him, he'll be confused. If you acknowledge
him, he'll follow you.

                              FIONA
That sounds like a him problem.

                              TESS
It becomes a you problem when he starts appearing places.

                              FIONA
People appear places all the time.

                              TESS
Not the same places. Not repeatedly. Not like a lost golden
retriever.

          FIONA shakes her head, but she's smiling now.

                              FIONA
I cannot believe this is a real conversation.

                              TESS
I'm just trying to protect you.

                              FIONA
From… eye contact?

                              TESS
From consequences.

                              FIONA
The consequence of looking at someone is not ownership.

                              TESS
Tell that to the ducks and the puppies.

                              FIONA
I hate that you might be right on all this.

                            TESS

Thank you.

> *TESS checks her reflection again, then looks at
> FIONA.*

                            TESS

Just, next time, blink more. Break it up.

                            FIONA

Break up my eye contact by blinking? Gimme a break, Tess.

                            TESS

Fine. But when he's following you down the hallway,
wagging his tail, panting and begging for treats, don't say I
didn't warn you.

                            FIONA

If he does any of that, I'm calling security.

                            TESS

You can't call security on your own imprint!

                            FIONA

Watch me annotate that.

> *Bell rings.*

                            FIONA

We're late.

                            TESS

Again.

> *They grab their things as SAGE and SOPHIA re-
> enter.*

FIONA

(to SOPHIA and SAGE) That was the bell!

SOPHIA

Not ours, we're seniors.

TESS

Come on, Fiona!

TESS and FIONA exit.

SCENE 3

SAGE

Also – college stuff. If your mom is like my mom, then she's probably asking how many scholarships you've breathed near today.

SOPHIA

My mom printed the FAFSA.

SAGE

Oh my gah. In color, right?

SOPHIA

In a binder.

SAGE

A festive binder, I hope.

SOPHIA

A festive binder.

SOPHIA checks her phone again, then immediately pretends she did not.

                              SAGE

Still nothing?

                             SOPHIA

He's probably just – I don't know. Busy.

                              SAGE

With what? Lunch is not a job.

                             SOPHIA

Boys can be busy.

                              SAGE

Yes. Busy being emotionally unavailable.

                             SOPHIA

Maybe he's just not checking his phone. Maybe boys don't
do that.

                              SAGE

Gimme a break, guys are on their phones just as much as
girls are, so.

                             SOPHIA

(flicks water at SAGE) Chill, Sage.

                              SAGE

Stop.

                             SOPHIA

Ooooh! I'm melting!

          *SOPHIA smiles again, then catches herself and
          looks serious.*

SOPHIA

Do you ever think… maybe we're not actually friends with anyone?

SAGE

That escalated.

SOPHIA

No, I mean – like. Everyone's "friends." But it's also like… who's real?

SAGE

Are you okay?

SOPHIA

I'm fine. I'm just – it's December. People get weird in December, okay? Gimme a break.

SAGE

Because of the holidays.

SOPHIA

Holidays and because there's like, glitter everywhere and you can't escape it, and everyone's pretending to be happy while also trying not to fail Pre-Calc.

SAGE

Mr. Redding is personally ruining the holiday spirit.

SOPHIA

Mr. Redding ruins life. He assigned a take-home quiz over Thanksgiving.

SAGE

He's like a math villain.

A beat. SOPHIA looks at her reflection. She's almost about to say something real.

                    SOPHIA
I'm not going to the winter dance.

                    SAGE
You say that every year.

                    SOPHIA
This year I mean it.

                    SAGE
Why?

                    SOPHIA
Because – it's stupid.

                    SAGE
Everything's stupid. That's not a reason.

                    SOPHIA
Because I don't want to stand there under the stupid snowflake lights while stupid people take stupid pictures and then I have to see myself from stupid angles I didn't consent to.

                    SAGE
That is… actually a reason.

                    SOPHIA
Thank you.

                    SAGE
Stupid, but. *(beat)* But, Soph, you always look good, come on, girl.

SOPHIA

No. I look good in mirrors. I do not look good in photos.

SAGE

Nobody looks good in photos taken by freshmen with shaky hands and crappy cameras.

SOPHIA

Makayla looks good in photos.

SAGE

Makayla looks good in security camera footage.

SOPHIA

Right?

> *SAGE watches SOPHIA carefully. She is clocking something. She chooses not to press – yet.*

SAGE

Is this about Emerson?

SOPHIA

No.

SAGE

Soph.

SOPHIA

It is not about Emerson.

SAGE

Okay.

> *SOPHIA checks her phone again. Buzz – nothing. She exhales through her nose, like she's mad at herself for caring.*

                         SOPHIA
It's just – if he wanted to, he would.

                         SAGE
That phrase is destroying a generation. No, wait; that's
phones and social media.

                         SOPHIA
It's true though.

                         SAGE
Sometimes. Sometimes people are just… people.

          *SOPHIA'S phone vibrates with a distinct pattern.
          She freezes.*

                         SAGE
What?

                         SOPHIA
Nothing.

                         SAGE
Sophia.

                         SOPHIA
It's – it's just a notification.

                         SAGE
From who?

                         SOPHIA
From… everyone, apparently.

          SAGE'S phone vibrates with the same pattern.

                         SAGE
Okay, that's weird.

SOPHIA

Why is it doing that?

Bell rings.

SOPHIA

(referring to bell) That's not ours.

SAGE

It's Halpern emailing us about Friday.

SOPHIA

If Mr. Halpern is emailing me during lunch, I'm transferring.

SAGE

Nobody transfers during December. The counselors would faint.

They both look at their screens without showing each other; they see, but they don't share. The silence is a dodge.

SOPHIA

It's probably nothing.

SAGE

It's never nothing when phones do that.

SOPHIA

These group chats are killing me.

SAGE

Group? More like the whole school.

SOPHIA

It could be something about the homecoming theme vote.

SAGE

Homecoming was in October.

SOPHIA

I mean winter dance. The theme. The "Snowed In" versus "Candy Cane Lane."

SAGE

No one is fighting about "Candy Cane Lane."

SOPHIA

Freshmen are. Freshmen fight about air.

SAGE

True.

SCENE 4

GABRIELA bursts in, one hand clamped over her right eye. FIONA – her confidant – follows.

GABRIELA

I'm blind.

FIONA

You're not blind.

SAGE

Oh my gah! What are you two doing?

SOPHIA

Do you have a hall pass?

FIONA

It's lunch!

GABRIELA

I'm spiritually and optically blind.

SOPHIA

What is wrong with her?

GABRIELA

It folded.

SOPHIA

What folded?

FIONA

Can we get to the sink, please?

GABRIELA

My contact. It taco'd.

FIONA

Don't say it like that!

SAGE

Let's get out of here, Soph.

SOPHIA

Isn't there supposed to be a lockdown drill today?

SAGE and SOPHIA exit.

GABRIELA

It's folded in my eye, Fiona. It's like a soft tortilla of suffering.

FIONA

Contacts don't tortilla.

GABRIELA

This one did. I felt it. It creased like a tiny transparent
napkin.

FIONA

You still have the other eye.

GABRIELA

That's not how binocular vision works. This is a crisis.

GABRIELA turns faucet on, bends over the sink.

GABRIELA

It's migrating.

FIONA

I can't believe you are running that nasty school water in
your face.

GABRIELA

I can't help it, Fiona! I'm dying!

FIONA

Come on. Look up.

GABRIELA

(stands straight) I am looking up.

FIONA

Not at me! At the ceiling. *(beat)* Stop looking at me like I'm
judging you.

GABRIELA

You are judging me.

FIONA

Gabby, I'm assessing the situation *(puts a finger under GABRIELA'S eye)*. Oh, I see it.

GABRIELA

Is it plotting?

FIONA

It's crumpled.

GABRIELA

Like my GPA after chemistry.

FIONA

Focus. Stop being dramatic.

GABRIELA

I narrate when I'm stressed.

FIONA

You narrate when you're bored, happy, hungry –

GABRIELA

Don't make me laugh. It hurts when I laugh. My cornea is compromised.

TESS enters.

TESS

Oh my gah, is she sick?

GABRIELA

Who is that?

FIONA

Tess.

GABRIELA

Hi, Tess. I'm dying.

FIONA

She's not dying! Her contact got folded or something.

GABRIELA

Do something, Fiona!

TESS does a quick mirror-check, goes into a stall.

FIONA adjusts the water to a gentler stream.

FIONA

Okay. We're flooding it.

GABRIELA

That sounds violent.

FIONA

It's hydration *(moves GABRIELA'S head toward sink)*. Tilt
your head.

GABRIELA

If this is how I go, tell people I was brave.

FIONA

I will not lie.

GABRIELA

I felt it move. Oh, gah Fiona!

FIONA

In a good way or a horror-movie way?

GABRIELA

In a way that suggests it has a life of its own.

FIONA

A little alien in your eye!

GABRIELA

It wants freedom.

FIONA

It wants oxygen.

GABRIELA

Same.

> *GABRIELA steadies herself, pinches delicately at her eye.*

GABRIELA

If I scream, assume it's victory.

FIONA

That's not how screaming –

GABRIELA

GOT IT.

> *GABRIELA straightens, holding up the tiny folded lens between triumphant fingers.*

GABRIELA

Behold. The villain, Iago.

FIONA

Iago, the contact lens. Oh my gah. It's so small.

GABRIELA

Small but malicious. Look at that crease. That's intentional.

FIONA

It's physics.

GABRIELA

It's betrayal.

She accidentally drops it into the sink. Both freeze.

FIONA

Did you just –

GABRIELA

It's fine.

FIONA

It's in the sink.

GABRIELA

I will disinfect it.

TESS

(comes out of stall) The sink is gross. *(Another mirror-check, exits.)*

FIONA

Please tell me you have solution.

GABRIELA

In my bag.

FIONA

Where's your bag?

GABRIELA

English.

FIONA

Of course.

GABRIELA
Mr. Baines believes leaving class is a moral failure.

FIONA
He thinks blinking is a sign of weakness – something, I've been told, I should actually do more often.

GABRIELA
He demands eye contact. I almost told him that's ironic.

GABRIELA blinks experimentally.

GABRIELA
Okay. I can see. Slightly pink. Slightly betrayed. But functional.

FIONA
Congratulations on retaining your sight.

GABRIELA
That sucked.

FIONA
C'mon, let's go. I'm starving.

GABRIELA
Oh my gah, look at my hair.

FIONA
Let's go!

GABRIELA
Wait, did she say there's a lockdown drill today?

FIONA
They announced it this morning, Gabby. Let's go!

SCENE 5

SOPHIA and SAGE re-enter.

SAGE
(looking at FIONA and GABRIELA) Whoa.

SOPHIA
Her contact still?

GABRIELA
We got it. We're leaving. Is there a lockdown drill today?

SAGE
That's what they said.

FIONA
See? Let's go *(exits)*.

GABRIELA
(exiting) That was awful.

SOPHIA
(resuming earlier issues) Okay, I'm not looking.

SAGE
You already looked.

SOPHIA
I glanced.

SAGE
That counts as looking.

SOPHIA
I didn't read.

                         SAGE

Sophia.

                         SOPHIA

Sage.

          *They stare again. It's funny and tense at the same
          time.*

                         SAGE

On a scale of one to "Principal Walters is calling an
assembly," how bad is it?

                         SOPHIA

I don't know.

                         SAGE

Read it.

                         SOPHIA

I don't want to read it in a bathroom.

                         SAGE

Where else? This is where we live.

          *Beat. SOPHIA inhales, steels herself, and finally
          reads. Her face shifts – just a little.*

                         SOPHIA

Oh.

                         SAGE

What?

                         SOPHIA

Nothing.

                    SAGE
Sophia.

                    SOPHIA
It's – probably fake.

                    SAGE
What is?

                    SOPHIA
It's just – people are being people.

                    SAGE
Tells me nothing.

                    SOPHIA
I don't want to say it.

                    SAGE
You don't have to say it. Show me.

> *SOPHIA hesitates, then angles the phone slightly –
> still guarded. SAGE reads. Her calm changes too,
> but she contains it.*

                    SAGE
Okay.

                    SOPHIA
Okay, like…okay, "okay"?

                    SAGE
Okay, like…this is going to be a problem.

                    SOPHIA
Right. *(deflecting)* Maybe it's old.

                    SAGE

It's time-stamped.

                    SOPHIA

Time-stamps can be wrong.

                    SAGE

No, they can't.

                    SOPHIA

Maybe it's AI.

                    SAGE

Not everything is AI.

                    SOPHIA

Everything is AI now.

                    SAGE

No. People still make bad choices on their own.

                    SOPHIA
(her humor drains) Who would do that?

                    SAGE

Don't.

                    SOPHIA

Don't what?

                    SAGE

Don't start naming people. Not yet.

                    SOPHIA

I'm not naming people.

SAGE

Your eyes are naming people.

SOPHIA

(looks away, ashamed that she's already spiraling) This is –
this is not – this is –

SAGE

I know.

SOPHIA

What time is it?

SAGE

12:17.

SOPHIA

It's literally 12:17?

SAGE

Yep.

SOPHIA

So we still have –

SAGE

Two hours until last bell.

SOPHIA

Oh my gah.

SAGE

Okay. Breathe. We're not doing the thing where we panic in
a bathroom and then walk out like it's normal and then pass
out in the hallway.

 Bell rings.

SOPHIA

I'm losing track of the bells. *(beat)* And hey, I don't pass out.

SAGE

You almost passed out during the PSAT.

SOPHIA

That was because the proctor wouldn't let me have water.

SAGE

And because you didn't eat breakfast.

SOPHIA

I had a granola bar.

SAGE

In the parking lot.

SOPHIA

Still counts. *(phone buzzes)* I hate this.

SAGE

Me too *(grabs paper towel to wipe water from dispenser)*.
Okay, here's what we're not
doing.

SOPHIA

Okay.

SAGE

We're not spreading it.

SOPHIA

I'm not spreading it.

SAGE

We're not sending it to anyone "just to see."

SOPHIA

I wouldn't.

SAGE

We're not making jokes.

SOPHIA

I'm not –

SAGE

We're not blaming –

SOPHIA

Not blaming –

SAGE

(they freeze) We're not doing that.

SOPHIA

Okay *(eyes fill with tears a little, but she refuses to let it happen)*. I need to go back out there.

SAGE

Why?

SOPHIA

Because if I stay in here I'm going to start thinking and then I'm going to cry and then my mascara is going to be –

SAGE

Okay!

SOPHIA

Okay?

                                SAGE

Okay. We go out like normal. We don't act weird. We don't
act like we know more than we know. We keep our eyes
open.

                               SOPHIA

Sounds like a spy movie.

                                SAGE

High school is a spy movie. Just with crappy lighting.

          They almost laugh.

                               SOPHIA

Do you think Mr. Halpern knows?

                                SAGE

Mr. Halpern doesn't know what day it is. Except maybe
"Friday."

                               SOPHIA

Friday.

                                SAGE

Friday.

                               SOPHIA

(another buzz) Okay, but – Sage.

                                SAGE

Yeah?

                               SOPHIA

What if this is… big?

          *SAGE looks at SOPHIA in the mirror. For the first
          time, she lets the seriousness show.*

SAGE

It is. I think it is big.

> *They stand there. Two girls. A bathroom. A world outside the door that is about to change. From the hallway, a burst of laughter; then a hush, as if laughter got swallowed.*

SOPHIA

I hate that sound.

SAGE

Me too *(goes to door)*. Ready?

SOPHIA

No.

SAGE

Me neither.

SCENE 6

> *TESS bursts in followed by BRENNA already mid-sentence.*

SOPHIA

Watch it! *(exits)*

BRENNA

Sorry.

SAGE

Gimme a break. Stupid freshmen. *(exits)*

BRENNA

We're not freshmen!

SAGE

(from offstage) Whatever.

BRENNA

(to SAGE and SOPHIA) We're not freshmen!

TESS

Delete it.

BRENNA

I'm not deleting it.

TESS

Delete it!

BRENNA

You said it was funny.

TESS

That was before I saw my face.

BRENNA

Your face is always your face.

TESS

Exactly.

> *TESS lunges for BRENNA's phone. BRENNA spins away.*

BRENNA

Relax. It's just the vape.

TESS

It's not just the vape. I look like I'm inhaling a ghost.

BRENNA
(laughing) You were inhaling a ghost.

TESS
It was gross and my mom will kill me.

BRENNA
Your mom doesn't even know what vaping looks like.

TESS
She has Facebook.

BRENNA
Okay, that's fair.

TESS
You did it, too.

BRENNA
(she's not in the video) And where am I in the video?

Phones buzz in same pattern as earlier. Both freeze.

TESS
Why is everyone's phone going off today?

BRENNA
It's lunch.

TESS
It's different.

Same phone buzz pattern.

BRENNA
That's the senior group chat vibration.

                    TESS

How do you know that?

                    BRENNA

I know things.

                    TESS

You're a junior.

                    BRENNA

I'm socially advanced.

> *They both look at their screens. Their faces shift. Not shocked. Recalibrating.*

                    TESS

Oh.

                    BRENNA

Yeah.

                    TESS

That's not –

                    BRENNA

It's real.

                    TESS

Is it though?

                    BRENNA

It's gotta be everywhere.

                    TESS
(grabs BRENNA's arm) is that – ?

                    BRENNA

Yes.

                    TESS

No.

                    BRENNA

Yeah.

                    TESS

Okay, but – that's not even –

                    BRENNA

I know.

                    TESS

You can't even –

                    BRENNA

I know.

> *They both look at the door instinctively, like someone might walk in.*
>
> *Bell rings.*

                    TESS

That's a second lunch bell. Who sent it?

                    BRENNA

Does it matter?

                    TESS

Yes.

                    BRENNA

No.

TESS

(buzz) Oh my gah it's in the sophomore chat now.

BRENNA

Already?

TESS

It says 12:17.

BRENNA

That was like five seconds ago.

TESS

It spreads fast. *(considers her own issue)* It's something you send and then it's not yours
anymore.

BRENNA

This is… *(realizes)* awful. Think about it. It's not even that it spreads. It's that it changes shape while it's spreading. Like in middle school when that rumor went around that I cried in math class. I didn't cry. I had something in my eye. But by third period I was "unstable." By fifth period I was "having a breakdown." By the bus it was "Brenna can't handle pressure."

And I just kept thinking – that's not what happened. That's not what it was. But it didn't matter anymore what it was. It mattered what it became.

And once something becomes a story, you don't get to edit it. Other people do. They add tone. They add emojis. They add their own angle.

And then one day you walk into a room and everyone's looking at you like they've read something you didn't write.

I didn't even cry. But this? This is bigger.

                          TESS
(moves to the full-length mirror) She's gonna die.

                        BRENNA
She's not gonna die.

                          TESS
Socially.

                        BRENNA
She's Makayla.

                          TESS
Exactly.

          *They both know what that means. If it can happen to
          MAKAYLA…*

                        BRENNA
Maybe it's a fake.

                          TESS
It's not fake.

                        BRENNA
You don't know that.

                          TESS
It's her.

                        BRENNA
Okay but it's not even that kind of –

                          TESS
I know.

                          BRENNA
You can't even see –

                          TESS
I know.

          Silence. Buzz. Buzz.

                          TESS
Oh my gah, someone sent it with the snowflake emoji.

                          BRENNA
That's stupid.

                          TESS
It's December.

                          BRENNA
It's not funny.

          TESS looks like she might cry, but she's fighting it.

                          TESS
Delete mine.

                          BRENNA
Tess –

                          TESS
Delete it! Please.

          *BRENNA hesitates. Then she opens her phone,
          swipes, then hits a button.*

                          BRENNA
Okay.

TESS

(buzz) Oh my gah it's in the girls' chat now.

BRENNA

Of course it is.

TESS

It says, "don't open in class."

BRENNA

We're not in class.

TESS

That's worse.

BRENNA

Okay. We're not sending it.

TESS

I didn't send it.

BRENNA

We're not reacting to it either.

TESS

How do you not react to that?

BRENNA

Just – act normal.

TESS

Makayla won't. *(long buzz)* Someone said Principal Walters knows.

BRENNA

No way. How?

                           TESS

It says "Walrus is calling people down."

                         BRENNA

People say stupid things.

                           TESS

It's moving.

                         BRENNA

Okay, we didn't see anything.

                           TESS

We saw it.

                         BRENNA

We didn't see it!

                           TESS

Brenna. Delete mine.

                         BRENNA

But you just saw me.

                           TESS

I don't think you actually deleted it.

SCENE 7

> *ILAN enters, scanning her phone. She moves like someone who thinks before she speaks. MIA; quieter, more detached, follows a beat later.*

                           ILAN

Oh, great. Mom just texted me three paragraphs about "focus."

                           MIA

That's short for her. *(to BRENNA)* Can I get here, please?

                         BRENNA

Sure.

                           TESS

Oh, my gah. Hi Mia, hi Ilan! *(to BRENNA)* Let's go.

                           MIA

Oh, hi Brenna! I didn't know that was you.

                         BRENNA

It's me, girl.

                           MIA

I love your top. Bye!

                         BRENNA

Thanks, girl! Bye!

                           MIA

I love yours, too, Tess!

          BRENNA and TESS exit.

          Bell rings.

                          ILAN

Her text had bullet points.

                           MIA

Who's?

                          ILAN

My mom's.

                              MIA

Bullet points?

                              ILAN

One: Grades. Two: Discipline. Three: Future.

                              MIA

In that order?

                              ILAN

In bold.

                              MIA

Like she's shouting. What did you do?

                              ILAN

I got an 88.

                              MIA

On what?

                              ILAN

Existence. *(beat)* Pre-Calc.

                              MIA

That's not even bad.

                              ILAN

In my house it's a public statement *(tosses her phone hard
into her bag)*. She said, "you're capable of more."

                              MIA

Her favorite sentence.

                              ILAN

I know. Sounds nice. It's not.

                    MIA
But my grandma used to say that.

                    ILAN
Yeah?

                    MIA
But she meant it like, you don't have to rush.

                    ILAN
How's your mom?

                    MIA
Cleaning.

                    ILAN
Like, cleaning cleaning?

                    MIA
Like she's trying to erase something.

                    ILAN
You don't have to be back to normal.

                    MIA
Everyone else is.

                    ILAN
Everyone else isn't you.

            *A quick burst of noise from the hallway. Someone
            runs past, voices. Lockers slam.*

                    MIA
It's loud today.

ILAN

It's always loud.

MIA

It's different.

ILAN

Did you see that picture?

MIA

I think everyone has by now.

ILAN

Yeah.

MIA

It's weird.

ILAN

Weird is hardly the word I'd use. Halpern said something
yesterday.

MIA

Always something.

ILAN

No, about responsibility. *(remembers)* "The law measures
intention. Life measures impact."

MIA

That was about the Constitution.

    The bell rings, loud, sharp.

MIA

I hate that sound.

                            ILAN

Second bell coming up.

                           BRENNA

(bursts in) Oh, my gah, Mia, they're calling people to the
office.

                            ILAN

Who?

                           BRENNA

I don't know. Just – people. *(exits)*

                            ILAN

You coming?

          MIA looks at her phone. Small shift in her face.

                            ILAN

What?

                            MIA

The pattern. On the couch. It's just like my grandma's.

                            ILAN

Okay. I don't think anyone is looking at that.

                            MIA

The blue one. With the little gold lines. *(she swallows)* I used
to sleep on it when I was little.

                            ILAN

Mia, that doesn't –

                            MIA

I know. It just makes it feel like something got pulled out of
a room it didn't belong in.

Bell rings.

ILAN

We're late.

MIA

Let them mark me absent.

ILAN

You'll get an email. Your parents will get an email.

ILAN looks at the picture.

ILAN

(referring to the couch) This isn't yours. I'm so sorry about –
about what happened, Mia. To your grandma. I know you
were really close with her. I'm sorry. *(puts a hand on MIA'S
arm)* We're gonna be late.

MIA

I don't care.

ILAN

(beat) All right. I'll stay with you, but I gotta pee *(goes into
stall, closes the door – we do not hear any sound)*.

MIA

Nothing stays where it starts. You know? I used to think it
did. I used to think rooms were containers. Like if something
happened in a room, it belonged to that room. And even,
like, monsters.

ILAN

(from closed stall) What? Did you say monsters?

MIA

Yeah, like monsters can't move from room to room. Once you close the door, they're stuck in there. Like, the monster can't get you if the door's closed. Like the monster can't get you if the covers are over you in bed. *(beat)* My grandma's living room was blue and gold and quiet. The couch had that pattern that made you dizzy if you stared at it too long. And everything felt… held. Like everything was there because it was meant to be there.

When she got sick, people kept coming in and out and bringing casseroles and flowers and it stopped feeling like a room and started feeling like a hallway. Like things were passing through it instead of living there.

And now it's like that again. Something that was supposed to stay small – like inside a phone, inside a conversation, inside a second – just keeps moving. And every time it moves it changes shape a little. It's not even about what it is anymore. It's about how far it goes. How fast.

Halpern talks about intention like it's this clear thing. Like you can measure it. But impact isn't clean. It leaks. It sticks to things. It drags other stuff with it.

That couch was supposed to stay in that living room. That living room was supposed to stay with her. And now it's just… everywhere. Like a monster got out.

I don't think anything knows how to stay anymore.

ILAN

(from the stall) Mia. I can't believe you said all that. I think I'm gonna cry.

                              MIA

(beat) I can't believe you're peeing while I'm saying all this.
Please tell me you didn't do anything else.

                             ILAN

(steps out of stall) Almost.

                              MIA

Gross.

                             ILAN

I'm kidding. *(beat)* We should go.

                              MIA

You go. I need a minute.

                             ILAN

Okay. I really kinda have to. Love you, girl.

                              MIA

Love you.

        Bell rings.

                             ILAN

(opening the bathroom door) Text me.

                              MIA

I will.

        *ILAN exits. A half second of quiet before next
        entrance. MIA puts her hands to her face as if she's
        going to allow herself to cry.*

SCENE 8

        *The bathroom door bursts open. FIONA, TESS, and
        GABRIELA tumble in, mid-conversation.*

                    FIONA
I shouldn't have eaten that second slice.

                    TESS
You had three.

                    FIONA
Why would you say that out loud?

                  GABRIELA
My stomach is literally expanding.

                    TESS
Same.

                    FIONA
I have a food baby.

                  GABRIELA
I have twins.

          *They all instinctively turn sideways in the mirror.
          Sweaters lift slightly. Jeans adjusted.*

                    TESS
Look. It's showing. It's a boy everyone, aw, how cute.

                    MIA
It's not.

                    FIONA
Look, see there's his li'l –

                    MIA
That's just being alive.

GABRIELA

No, this is structural.

TESS

I can't go to class like this.

FIONA

Like what? With organs?

GABRIELA

My jeans are tight.

TESS

Because you dried them.

GABRIELA

Don't blame the dryer.

HAZELL

(enters) Sorry *(exits immediately)*.

GABRIELA

(referring to HAZELL) What was that?

TESS

(not unkind) Who was that?

> *Phones buzz, they pull them out immediately.*

FIONA

Okay, why is everyone's phone freaking out?

TESS

Group chat.

GABRIELA

Which one?

                    TESS

All of them.

          *They scroll their phones. Micro-reactions. Quick
          glances at each other.*

                    FIONA

Oh.

                    MIA

Don't.

                    TESS

I'm not saying anything.

                    FIONA

It's not even –

                    MIA

(sharper than intended) Tsch!

                    GABRIELA

Okay, but –

                    MIA

Just don't.

                    TESS

I feel gross.

                    FIONA

From…pizza?

                    TESS

Not pizza.

                    GABRIELA

It says 12:17.

                    FIONA

It's time-stamped.

                    TESS

That was like half an hour ago.

                    GABRIELA

I don't think she knows yet.

                    FIONA

Don't say that.

                    GABRIELA

I haven't seen her all day.

                    TESS

She was in that double-period thing.

                    GABRIELA

Schneider.

                    FIONA

So she doesn't have her phone.

                    MIA

She will.

                    TESS

This is why I don't send anything.

                    FIONA

You sent that video of you vaping.

                              TESS
That was different.

                            GABRIELA
Was it?

                              TESS
(beat) Okay, I didn't send it anymore after.

                             FIONA
No one said you did.

                            GABRIELA
Everyone's staring in the hallway.

                             FIONA
At her?

                            GABRIELA
At everyone.

> *Door opens. MAKAYLA enters. Silence and stillness.
> She's holding her Government folder, slightly
> drained from the makeup exam, but composed.*

                            MAKAYLA
Why are you all in here? Hall pass? *(silent beat)*

> *TESS flashes her hall pass.*

                            MAKAYLA
Did the bell ring already?

> *Everyone clusters to one side giving MAKAYLA
> space.*

                              TESS
Yeah.

MAKAYLA

Great *(sets her folder down, runs water on her hands)*. If Schneider takes off points for "clarity" again, I'm transferring.

No one responds.

MAKAYLA

You're right. Wasn't funny. *(reads the room)* What?

FIONA

Nothing.

GABRIELA

We ate too much.

TESS

Food baby.

MAKAYLA

(glances at their stomach-check poses) You're fine.

BRENNA and ILAN enter.

BRENNA

Oh my gah. What is everybody doing in here?

ILAN

We are in so much trouble if the monitor comes back.

MIA

We should go.

MAKAYLA pulls out her phone – she hasn't checked it in two hours – turns her back to the audience and puts her lower back against the sink. She scrolls once. Twice. The other girls watch for a reaction.

> *Boom. She turns to the audience, one hand on the*
> *sink to steady herself, the other holding her phone.*

MAKAYLA

Oh.

TESS

Mak –

> *MAKAYLA raises a hand. Not angry. Just "wait."*

FIONA

(beat) Who took it?

GABRIELA

Did anybody do anything to you?

TESS

I'm sorry.

MAKAYLA

(going numb) For what.

FIONA

It's not even that –

GABRIELA

You can't really –

TESS

I'm sure it wasn't supposed to –

MAKAYLA

How long? *(beat, then impatiently)* How long?

ILAN

Since 12:17.

MAKAYLA processes that. She nods once.

                    MAKAYLA
Okay.

                    FIONA
It's in, like… other chats.

                    MAKAYLA
Okay.

                    BRENNA
Principal Walters might know.

                    MAKAYLA
Okay.

                    TESS
Did you send it to –

                    MAKAYLA
Did I send it?

                    TESS
No, I didn't mean –

                    MAKAYLA
I know what you meant. *(quietly)* Everybody out. *(beat)*
Please.

Still no one moves.

                    MAKAYLA
(explodes) GET OUT!

> *They jump. FIONA grabs GABRIELA, they exit.*
> *BRENNA and ILAN exit. TESS backs toward the*
> *door. MIA lingers half a second longer – then goes.*

MAKAYLA stands perfectly still for a moment. Then she moves – fast. Pacing.

MAKAYLA

Okay. Okay. Okay.

She unlocks her phone. Scrolls. Scrolls. Scrolls.

MAKAYLA

Delete. Delete. Delete. *(beat)* You can't delete something that isn't yours.

She stops herself.

MAKAYLA

It's not that… *(she looks at her reflection)* You look the same. You look exactly the same. No big deal. This is manageable. We can manage this.

She starts typing. Stops. Deletes.

MAKAYLA

Who –

She sinks to the floor, to the side of the sink so the audience can see her.

MAKAYLA

I was in a room. I was in a room for two hours. I was in a room taking a test. It wasn't even supposed to – it wasn't supposed to leave. I can't believe this.

She hits a few buttons on her phone, then:

MAKAYLA

Hi, mom. *(pause)* I'm fine.
No, I just – *(bursts into tears)*
Remember last weekend? When I was hanging out with Sophia and Sage?

Some other guys came over.

Guys and girls.

Something happened.
It wasn't my fault. I didn't bring anything.
I'm not sure who did.
I had – there was drinking going on and I swear I didn't have much.
I know. I'm sorry. I'm sorry, mom.
I didn't mean to.

No. No, I know. The big deal was somebody took pictures.

Yes.
Yeah.
It was stupid, I know.
But somebody shared the pictures and there of some of me that – *(she can't finish her sentence)*
Now they're apparently all over the school.

In the bathroom.
At school.

Come get me, mom.
Please come get me.

> *She pulls her knees to her chest, her breath hitching.*
> *She presses her forehead into her knees.*
>
> *She stands. Looks in the mirror.*

MAKAYLA
You look the same. *(She quickly wipes a tear away.)* You look exactly the same. Somebody else put that in your hand.

*She laughs once – hollow. She opens her phone.
Scrolls. Stops. Locks it. Puts it on the sink counter.
She grips the sink.*

MAKAYLA

(whispers, trying to convince herself) It wasn't even that bad.
(She sinks back down to the floor.)

SCENE 9

*A soft knock at the door. MAKAYLA looks straight
out. Another knock. Gentle.*

DESANTIS

Makayla? It's Ms. DeSantis. *(beat)* Makayla? I'm coming in,
okay?

*The door opens slowly. DESANTIS enters. She does
not rush. She closes the door behind her. She takes
in the scene for a moment.*

DESANTIS

Hi. I heard you might need a minute.

MAKAYLA

Who told you?

DESANTIS

Does it matter?

MAKAYLA shakes her head.

DESANTIS

I'm not here to ask questions.

MAKAYLA

I don't know how it all –

                         DESANTIS

I know.

                         MAKAYLA

They're saying –

                         DESANTIS

(lowers herself to MAKAYLA'S level) They're saying a lot of
things. You don't have to explain anything right now.

                         MAKAYLA

It looks worse than it is.

                         DESANTIS

Doesn't change how it feels. Does it?

                         MAKAYLA

I didn't mean for –

                         DESANTIS

I'm not blaming you, Makayla. And look, intention and
impact aren't the same thing.

                         MAKAYLA

I was just… just –

                         DESANTIS

You were just being a teenager.

                         MAKAYLA

I called my mom. My mom's coming.

                         DESANTIS

Good. That's good. We're going to handle this one step at a
time.

MAKAYLA

(almost laughs) You can't delete something that's already everywhere.

DESANTIS

No. But everywhere can feel bigger than it is.

> *DESANTIS gently picks up MAKAYLA'S phone from sink counter and hands it back to her.*
>
> *Bell rings.*

DESANTIS

Right now, we just get you through this hour. *(beat)* Hey. Makayla? Look at me. *(she does)* Hey. Can I tell you something? *(MAKAYLA doesn't respond – that's permission enough.)* Something that happened to me? When I was, oh, fifteen or sixteen, I got cast in the school musical. It was a big deal. For me. I had never had a solo before. I practiced for weeks.

Opening night, I missed my entrance. Not by a second. Not by a beat. By an entire verse.

The orchestra kept playing. The other actors kept singing. And I just…wasn't there. I was in the wings, frozen. I don't even remember why. I just remember the heat in my face when I realized. And the audience – you know how audiences do that thing? That shift? That murmur? It felt like the entire building knew. The next day, someone posted about it. Not even mean. Just…factual. Teresa DeSantis forgot her solo. But it didn't stay factual. It became dramatic. It became humiliating. It became a story I didn't recognize. And for about a week, I thought that was who I was. The girl who froze. It wasn't the worst thing that's ever happened to anyone. It wasn't even the worst thing that's ever happened to me.

DESANTIS (CONT)
But when you're inside it – it feels like it's permanent. *(beat)*
It wasn't.

MAKAYLA
But, Ms. DeSantis. That's not the same. Someone posted
about you. Me? There's a picture. And I'm – I'm –

DESANTIS
I know. You don't have to say it. I know. I'm sorry. *(beat)*
And you're right. It's not the same. All I'm trying to say is –

MAKAYLA
You missed a song.

DESANTIS
I did.

MAKAYLA
This is – this is something I can't pull back. I can't walk
onstage tomorrow and sing it correctly and make it go away.

DESANTIS
No. But you also don't have to live in the version of the story
that other people are building.

MAKAYLA
They already built it.

DESANTIS
Stories get loud. Then they get old. Then they fade.

MAKAYLA
I don't know how that's going to happen.

A knock at the door. Quick. Urgent.

SOPHIA

(still hasn't entered) Makayla?

SAGE

(still hasn't entered) Makayla? It's us.

MAKAYLA

Can they come in?

DESANTIS nods.

MAKAYLA

Come in.

SOPHIA and SAGE enter quickly.

SOPHIA

Oh. Sorry. We didn't –

SAGE

We don't have a hall pass.

DESANTIS

It's okay.

SOPHIA

I'm so sorry.

DESANTIS

Tell you what. I'm going to let Sophia and Sage here talk with you while I go down to the office and see if your mom's here.

MAKAYLA

Okay.

DESANTIS exits, closing the door softly. Silence.

SCENE 10

SOPHIA

We tried to get to you sooner. I mean, before.

MAKAYLA

I was in a test.

SAGE

We know.

MAKAYLA

Who took it?

SAGE

We don't know.

MAKAYLA

You were there.

SOPHIA

So were, like, twenty other people.

SAGE

We told them not to take pictures. *(MAKAYLA glares at her)* We did.

SOPHIA

When the guys came in and started being loud, we told them to put their phones away. It was stupid. Remember?

SAGE

Emerson had his phone out. Alex too. And those girls from Westbrook.

SOPHIA

It wasn't like – it wasn't organized. It was just chaos. Music.
People yelling. Someone grabbed someone's phone and
everyone thought it was funny.

MAKAYLA

Funny.

SAGE

Not funny like this.

SOPHIA

You weren't even –

MAKAYLA

Even what?

SOPHIA

You weren't even – no one had anything to drink by then. I
don't think.

SAGE

Everybody was drinking.

SOPHIA

(possibly untrue) I wasn't.

SAGE

You know how people are. Nobody listens.

SOPHIA

You'd think that people would get it to not have their phones
out and to not take pictures or anything.

SAGE

But people were going into different rooms. And you were –
I don't know where you were. With Nick?

MAKAYLA

What does that mean?

SAGE

Nothing. I just meant –

MAKAYLA

No. Say it.

SOPHIA

(jumping in) It doesn't mean anything. You were just talking. That's all.

MAKAYLA

Talking. So I leave the room and suddenly I'm digital content.

SAGE

That's not fair.

MAKAYLA

Isn't it? You were right there!

SOPHIA

We were trying to keep things under control.

MAKAYLA

By what? Laughing?

SOPHIA

We weren't laughing.

SAGE

It didn't look like this yet.

MAKAYLA

When did it start looking like this? When did it cross from
"chaos" to this?

SOPHIA

Makayla –

MAKAYLA

You're both seniors. Those Westbrook girls are juniors and
sophomores. Alex is a sophomore. They don't know
anything. You do.

SOPHIA

We told them to put their phones away.

MAKAYLA

And when they didn't?

SAGE

What were we supposed to do? Tackle them?

MAKAYLA

Yeah.

SOPHIA

We didn't think it was going to – we didn't think they'd take
pictures and then send them –

MAKAYLA

You didn't think is what you didn't do.

SOPHIA

So, what? This is our fault?

SAGE

Gimme a break! No one thinks in those moments! No one
thought.

MAKAYLA

I thought! I thought you both would be watching out for me!

SAGE

How are we supposed to watch out for you? We were
drinking, too!

SOPHIA

Well, I…

SAGE

Oh, come on, Soph. You know you did so cut it out.

MAKAYLA

Who put that thing in my hand? Who took the picture?

SOPHIA

Look, we tried to tell them to not take pictures, but how are
we supposed to stop anyone from sending photos? If they
send them, they send them!

SAGE

Somebody grabbed someone's phone for all we know and
then took the picture! We don't know!

MAKAYLA

(beat) You know what's gonna happen now?

SOPHIA

No.

MAKAYLA

Yes you do. They're not gonna say, "somebody grabbed
someone's phone." They're going to say my name.

SAGE

Makayla, we'll tell people what actually happened.

MAKAYLA

And they'll listen? *(beat)* You let them look at me.

SOPHIA

We didn't.

MAKAYLA

Like that.

SAGE

Makayla, you were in a different room! We can't follow you around all night!

SOPHIA

We didn't know.

MAKAYLA

Exactly. I was just in a room. *(beat)* And now, I'm everywhere. You know what people say? They don't ask what he was doing or what he was drinking or why he didn't help. They say, "what was she wearing? Why did her parents let her go there? Did she say something she shouldn't have?"

SAGE

But. Makayla. You're not what they're making this.

MAKAYLA

It doesn't matter what I am! It matters what they can screenshot.

> *Lights shift. A kind of freeze settles over SOPHIA and SAGE.*

Do you remember middle school?

> *MAKAYLA walks downstage – ostensibly 'outside' the bathroom – she's in her own world,*

MAKAYLA (CONT)

The dress code board outside the office? The one with the
bullet points? "No exposed shoulders." "No visible straps."
"No shorts above fingertip length." "No leggings unless
covered." They had a ruler. They actually had a ruler.

Mrs. Donnelly would stand there in the hallway between
classes and just… scan. Like airport security. If your
collarbone showed too much: office. If your shorts rode up
when you sat down: office. If your body happened to exist in
a way that filled out a shirt: office.

Remember how Emma could wear the same tank top as
Jenna but only one of them got sent down? Because one of
them "developed early." Like that was a crime.

And the boys? They wore muscle shirts. They sagged their
pants. They wrote stuff on their arms. They wore hoodies in
May. They could dress like thugs and nobody cared. Nobody
measured them. Nobody pulled them aside and said, "You're
distracting."

It was us. We were the distraction. We were the problem.
Girls.

We were told to sit a certain way. Cross your legs. Don't lean
forward. Don't laugh too loud. Don't have an opinion that's
too strong. And everything else. Don't wear too much
makeup – but don't look tired. Don't look like you're trying
– but don't look like you're not.

And every time an incident with boys happened, someone
would dismiss it and say, "Boys will be boys." It was like a

MAKAYLA (CONT)

permission slip. They could do whatever they want. The rules for them were somehow… different.

Lights shift as she walks back to being 'inside' the bathroom. SOPHIA and SAGE move naturally.

And now there's a picture. And nobody's going to ask what he was doing. Or what he was drinking. Or who grabbed whose phone.

They're going to ask what I was wearing. How much I drank. Why I went into another room. It's the same ruler. Just somehow… different.

SOPHIA

Senior year isn't supposed to be like this.

SAGE

There's time yet. It'll get better. It's barely December.

SOPHIA

Yeah. We have another six months to really screw things up.

MAKAYLA

You think this lasts six months?

SAGE

Nothing at this school lasts six months.

MAKAYLA

Pictures do.

SOPHIA

Makayla –

MAKAYLA

And you know what the worst part is? Nobody even knows what actually happened.

SOPHIA

We told you that.

MAKAYLA

No. You told me guesses.

SOPHIA

Nick might.

SAGE

We weren't in the room.

MAKAYLA

Exactly! You weren't in the room!

SOPHIA

Mak –

MAKAYLA

I would have thought someone would walk in.

SAGE

What do you mean?

MAKAYLA

Just… someone. Someone who knew me. Someone who would say, "Okay, that's enough."

SOPHIA

Makayla, we didn't know –

MAKAYLA

I know.

                                SAGE
Then why are you –

                              MAKAYLA
Because I was in there by myself! Well, maybe not
completely by myself. And now apparently I'm everywhere.

                               SOPHIA
We're trying to help.

                              MAKAYLA
By telling me what everyone thinks happened?

                                SAGE
We're here now and we're telling you what people are
saying.

                              MAKAYLA
Yeah. That's the problem. Know what happens tomorrow?
Everyone starts telling the story.

                                SAGE
We'll say we don't know.

                              MAKAYLA
It won't matter. Once there's a picture, people think they
know everything.

                               SOPHIA
Pictures don't show everything.

                              MAKAYLA
No. But they show enough for people to pretend. *(picks up
her phone, shows the picture)* And this? This shows enough.
(beat) I need you to leave.

                              SOPHIA

Mak –

                             MAKAYLA

Please.

                              SAGE

(trying to be helpful) We're not going anywhere.

                             MAKAYLA

Yes. You are. I need five minutes where nobody is explaining
what happened to me.

                              SOPHIA

We're on your side.

                             MAKAYLA

(shouts) Then give me the room *(she sits on the floor)*!

                              SAGE

(beat) Okay.

        SAGE and SOPHIA start toward the door.

                             MAKAYLA

Sophia. Tomorrow when people ask what happened…

                              SOPHIA

Yeah?

                             MAKAYLA

Just remember… I was actually there. And somehow I'm the
only one who doesn't get to tell it.

        SAGE begins kneeling to hug MAKAYLA.

MAKAYLA

No! No, Sage. I *(pushes through her tears)* I just need – to be – alone – right now.

Beat. SAGE and SOPHIA aren't leaving.

MAKAYLA

Just please go.

SAGE and SOPHIA go slowly toward the door. They open it and exit.

MAKAYLA

(crying, devastated) Mom. Come quick. Come quick, get me, mom. Please.

MAKAYLA sobs quietly as the lights fade.

End of Act I

ACT II

SCENE 1

Same set as before. The following dialogue – spoken offstage – should be delivered in unison and repeated (if necessary) and grow louder and louder, until the bell rings signaling everyone to go abruptly quiet:

SAGE

(offstage) I have no idea what I'm going to do. I have no idea what college I'm going to go to. Everybody tells me to go to an in-state college but I just want to get away from this provincial, in-bred town where nobody can think beyond their own front yard. Go somewhere and learn something!

SOPHIA

(offstage) It's like, I have my older sister to deal with and live up to. My parents are so unfair. They treat her like she hung the moon. Like she can do no wrong. And she is good. She is smart but what do I have to be compared to her constantly? This nightmare is unending!

BRENNA

(offstage) Why is the guidance counselor trying to get me to take all these honors courses and regents courses and IB courses? Nobody cares about that anymore. All I hear is how grades are so inflated that it doesn't even matter if you have a 4.0 – you have to have a weighted 4.9 to get into the most local, basic college. I don't want to even think about college!

ILAN

(offstage) An 81. I can't believe I got an 81 on that stupid test! It's going to completely tank my average and it's all because I had to go my cousin's absurd birthday party where

ILAN (CONT)

they spent thousands of dollars as if she was getting married or something! I hate her and her rich parents!

MIA

(offstage) Everyone is just so loud all the time. Nobody stops and thinks about other people. It's always me, me, me. Nothing matters to anyone unless it happens to them. They have to experience hurt and loss for them to be considerate to others. Why can't people just be kind to others and let them be who they are? Just leave me alone!

FIONA

(offstage) Geometry and chemistry in the same year? What do they expect of us? And these teachers that I can't understand because they don't even try to modify their lessons to accommodate students who have any measure of difficulty dealing with things. And forget going for extra help. They only make time for that at seven o'clock in the morning – and I am not doing that!

GABRIELA

(offstage) Doesn't matter how hard I try. I do the best I can, mostly. Teachers are telling me what to do; my parents are telling me what to do; my friends are telling me what to do. When do I get to decide what's best for me? I hate this place.

TESS

(offstage) I can't do anything but practice. My day is completely loaded. I get up, I get ready for school, I get homework, I have about an hour to do homework when I get home but then my mom is on me about cleaning my room and helping with my little brother and then my dad is yelling at me saying that we have to go to my next thing in ten minutes. It is too much!

NICK

(offstage) I have no idea how I passed that test. Senior year is supposed to be a breeze that's what I took all those ridiculous AP, regents, and honors courses in junior year and now with sports and practice and games I have no time to even think about college but that's all anybody wants to talk to me about. I can't wait to graduate.

EMERSON

(offstage) Not sure how I'm supposed to focus with all that's going on at home. Any moment now I know they're going to get divorced. I just have to keep my head down. But all I'm supposed to do according just about everyone else is to keep my head up. If they didn't want the responsibility, why did they ever get together in the first place? Just enough already!

Bell rings loud and long. Silence.

Stall door opens slowly. HAZELL emerges. She moves toward the sink, as if she's looking in the mirror, to practice her public speaking speech. She puts her bag on the sink edge.

HAZELL

(pulls out her flashcards, takes a deep breath) Okay. *(speech mode)* In Shakespeare's *Hamlet*, there is a moment when Hamlet is trying to decide what to do about the truth he has discovered. *(breaks from speech mode)* Even if it was from a ghost. *(recomposing herself, back to speech mode)* He knows something is wrong in the kingdom, but he also knows that what something *looks like* is not always what it really *is*.

And that's where the famous question comes from: "To be, or not to be." *(she forgets what come next, looks at her flashcard)* 'Most people,' I knew it. C'mon, Hazell. *(resumes speech mode)*

HAZELL (CONT)

Most people think that line is just about life and death. But it's really about choice. *(rethinks her delivery)* It's really about choice. *(her mind drifts)* Choice.

(resumes speech mode) Hamlet is asking himself whether he should act or not act. Whether he whether he should accept what everyone else believes… or challenge it.

And the reason that moment matters is because choice reveals character. If Hamlet had no choice – if someone forced him to act, or forced him to stay quiet – then the story wouldn't tell us anything about who he is. It would just tell us what happened to him.

But because he has a choice, we learn something deeper. We learn who he becomes. *(tries the line again with a hand gesture, steps 'out' of bathroom and toward audience, lights shift)* We learn who he becomes.

In the play, things are constantly pretending to be something they're not. People spy on each other. People lie. People perform roles. Something that looks true might actually be false. Something that looks harmless might actually be dangerous.

Shakespeare keeps asking the audience the same question: What is real? And maybe even more important: Who gets to decide what's real? That question matters because sometimes a story forms around a person before that person even has a chance to speak.

People see something. Or *think* they see something. And suddenly they believe they understand everything about what happened.

HAZELL (CONT)

But seeing something isn't the same as knowing it. And hearing a story isn't the same as understanding it. Choice is what gives a person the chance to say: "This is who I am." *(more firmly)* This. Is who. I am.

(glances quickly at her flashcard, then back toward audience) Not who someone else thinks they are. Not who a rumor says they are. Not who a moment makes them look like.

But who they choose to be.

> *BRENNA, GABRIELA and FIONA quietly enter the bathroom and watch – they are not in the main light.*

Because without that choice – without the chance to speak, or act, or decide – then a person isn't really living their own story. They're just living inside someone else's version of it.

And that might be the real tragedy in *Hamlet*.

Not that terrible things happen. But that sometimes the truth gets buried under what things look like. And once people believe the appearance… it can be very hard to change the reality.

SCENE 2

BRENNA

(after HAZELL'S moment has settled) Who… are you talking to?

HAZELL

(recomposes herself quickly, picks up her bag from sink) Oh! Sorry!

FIONA

Brenna, don't be mean!

> *HAZELL spills her notecards on the floor, scrambles to pick them up.*

GABRIELA

Oh my gah.

BRENNA

I wasn't being mean!

FIONA

(to HAZELL) It's okay, we were just asking. *(to BRENNA, somewhat annoyed)* Brenna.

BRENNA

What?

HAZELL

Sorry *(exits)*.

BRENNA

(beat) What?

FIONA

Don't be mean!

BRENNA

I wasn't being mean!

GABRIELA

It's okay, relax.

BRENNA

I was legitimately asking who she was talking to!

FIONA

I know, it's just. Just that girl is so shy, I didn't want to upset her.

BRENNA

But it seems like now you're getting mad at me!

FIONA

I just. *(beat)* People don't know how to just stop for a minute and think about how their actions might affect other people.

BRENNA

Are you saying that I don't think?

GABRIELA

No, Brenna.

FIONA

I'm just thinking out loud. And I yeah, I guess I am saying that you didn't think –

BRENNA

Fiona!

FIONA

No, I mean that in a nice way!

BRENNA

How is that nice?

FIONA

I mean that it's something we all do. Me included!

GABRIELA

Yeah, we sometimes just burst in on a situation and don't think before we speak – we just speak.

BRENNA
Well, I didn't mean to upset her or sound mean.

FIONA
No one ever does. But that's my point.

BRENNA
(beat) So what am I supposed to do? Never say anything?
Go out in the hallway and retrieve her?

FIONA
No. Just… maybe look first.

BRENNA
Look at what?

FIONA
The room. The person. The moment. *(beat)* Sometimes
people are in the middle of something.

BRENNA
I didn't know she was. She was talking like there was
somebody in here or she was onstage or something.

GABRIELA
Maybe she was practicing.

BRENNA
In the bathroom?

GABRIELA
Where else is she gonna practice?

BRENNA
I guess. *(beat)* I mean, she sounded good. Smart.

GABRIELA

Yeah. I think she is. My mom says still waters run deep.

BRENNA

I guess. I mean, I didn't understand half of what she was saying, but it sounded important.

FIONA

It did.

BRENNA

We just walked in at the wrong moment.

GABRIELA

Yeah.

BRENNA

I hate that feeling.

FIONA

What feeling?

BRENNA

When you realize you said something and the room changes. Like suddenly everyone hears it differently than you meant it.

GABRIELA

You didn't mean anything by it.

BRENNA

That doesn't really matter though, does it?

FIONA

Sometimes it does.

BRENNA

Sometimes it doesn't. Sometimes it just... sticks there.
Like... gum.

GABRIELA

Gum? Gum? That's a terrible metaphor!

BRENNA

You know what I mean. *(beat)* Do you think she thinks I'm
awful?

FIONA

No.

BRENNA

You answered that way too fast.

FIONA

I'm serious. But maybe next time just say something like –

GABRIELA

Like, "Hey, sorry, didn't mean to interrupt."

Bell rings.

BRENNA

I didn't interrupt!

GABRIELA

You kinda did.

BRENNA

Okay. Fine. Next time.

FIONA

(beat) Why are we in here again?

BRENNA

Right. My lip gloss.

GABRIELA

My contacts.

FIONA

I gotta pee.

GABRIELA

We're gonna be late.

BRENNA

(applying gloss; slightly open mouth, trying to keep lips as still as possible) Fixing lips.

GABRIELA

We're gonna be late.

FIONA

(going into stall) I gotta pee.

SCENE 3

MIA enters the bathroom.

MIA

Oh, hey, Gabby.

GABRIELA

Hey, Mia. *(beat)* The bell's gonna ring.

MIA

I know. I got a hall pass. Hey, Brenna.

BRENNA

(finishing her lip gloss) Hey, girl.

MIA

Who else is in here?

FIONA

(from inside stall) Hey, Mia! I'm peeing.

ILAN enters.

ILAN

Oh my gah, what's going on in here?

BRENNA

(through pursed lips) Girl.

GABRIELA

We've been through this. Brenna is doing her lips, I'm fixing my contacts and Fiona is peeing.

FIONA

(still from inside stall, elongated) Hey.

GABRIELA

Got it. All right, y'all, I'm gone *(exits)*.

BRENNA

That'll do. Bye! See you last period *(exits)*.

MIA

Bye!

Bell rings.

ILAN

(to MIA) I'm so glad you're here.

MIA

What is it?

ILAN

I just came from Salisbury's room and she's already talking about the next test.

MIA

Already?

ILAN

Already. Like the last one didn't just destroy my life.

MIA

At least she's nice though.

ILAN

Who cares? A test's a test.

FIONA

(emerges from stall) Oh my gah, I gotta go! *(mirror check, then)* Bye!

ILAN AND MIA:

(not simultaneously) Bye!

MIA

What did you get?

ILAN

On what?

MIA

The last test!

ILAN

89.

MIA

Oh my gah, that's so good!

ILAN

Not in my house. An 89 is basically a public apology.

MIA

My grandma used to say 89 was a lucky number.

ILAN

How is 89 a lucky number?

MIA

Well, she said that about any number grade I got. *(missing her grandmother)* Still, she didn't believe that numbers told the whole story. Like, we focus too much on grades and numbers and achievement and involvement.

ILAN

Tell that to my parents. Every conversation in my house is the same. 'What did you get? What could you have done better? What's your plan?'

MIA

That sounds exhausting.

ILAN

It is exhausting. And the worst part is, I usually agree with them. Like, I know I could've done better. So then I'm mad at them for saying it, but I'm also mad at myself for proving them right. It's like living with a panel of judges.

TESS enters, breathless.

TESS

Is anyone in here?

ILAN

Just us.

                          TESS

Okay.

                           MIA

What is it?

                          TESS

Nothing. Everything. Do you ever feel like the whole school
is just… watching?

                          ILAN

Today? Yes.

                          TESS

No, I mean, all the time. Like you're always one moment
away from doing something embarrassing.

                           MIA

Sounds stressful.

                          TESS

It is *(pulls out her phone, glances, puts it away quickly)*.

                          ILAN

What?

                          TESS

Nothing.

                           MIA

Tess.

                          TESS

(hesitates, then) Everyone keeps sending things.

                          ILAN

Yeah.

                              TESS

And my phone was in my hand. And I almost sent it, too.

                              ILAN

But you didn't.

                              TESS

No. But I thought about it. And the weird part is I wasn't
even thinking about the person in it.

                              ILAN

Okay. What were you thinking about?

                              TESS

Just… being part of it. Like if everyone else is doing
something, you start thinking maybe it's normal.

                              MIA

Happens a lot.

                              TESS

Yeah. And then I realized something.

                              ILAN

What?

                              TESS

If I send it, I'm part of the story. Part of the problem. And if I
don't send it… I'm still part of the story. The problem.

                              MIA

Why?

                              TESS

Because I saw it. So now I know.

MIA

My grandma used to say something like that. Like, she said once you know something about a person, you have to decide what kind of person you're going to be about it. That it's a choice. You know, like Ms. McKenna says we are the sum total of our choices?

TESS

That's… a lot of responsibility.

ILAN

Your grandma sounds smarter than my entire family.

MIA

She also believed that grief makes you kinder. If you let it in.

ILAN

Do you think that's true?

MIA

I hope so. I want to be thought of as a kind person.

TESS

You are.

MIA

Remember that unit in social studies when we talked about grief? The were, like, five stages, I think. By Kübler-Ross.

ILAN

Such a weird name. I'll never forget it. Like Kubla Kahn, or something.

MIA

What were they? Denial, anger, bargaining…

ILAN AND TESS

Depression and acceptance.

MIA

Ms. Symons wrote them on the board like it was a timeline… like if you just follow the steps you eventually arrive somewhere neat and organized. But I don't think grief works like that.

When my grandmother died, I thought I understood what those stages meant. I thought denial meant you say, "This isn't happening." I thought anger meant yelling. I thought acceptance meant you're finally okay. But it's not like that.

Sometimes denial is just waking up in the morning and forgetting for a second. Just one second. And then remembering again.

And anger isn't yelling. Sometimes it's just this quiet feeling that the world kept moving when it shouldn't have.

And acceptance… I'm not even sure that's the right word. Because it's not like you accept that someone is gone. You just slowly learn how to carry them in a different way. My grandmother used to say grief is love that doesn't know where to go anymore.

I think that's why it hurts so much.

Because the love is still there. It's just… looking for a place to land.

TESS

Oh, Mia. I'm so sorry about your grandma. What you said was so beautiful. And sad.

ILAN

This is going to sound weird but what you said reminds me of that painting by Picasso. With the dark blue sky, the stars and swirls over the little village. So peaceful. What's the name of it?

MIA

It reminds you of a painting?

ILAN

Yeah, I know, right? *(remembers)* Oh, Starry Night, I think.

TESS

Starry Night isn't Picasso, Ilan. It's Van Gogh.

ILAN

Whatever.

TESS

Way to ruin the moment, Ilan.

MIA

Not even an 89.

ILAN

Gimme a break. Just cos I don't know every artist in the world.

MIA

I'm teasing, Ilan. Relax.

TESS

(beat) I think I'm still deciding what kind of person I am.

ILAN

Welcome to high school.

                              MIA

Welcome to being alive.

                              TESS

Do you ever wish people would just… pause?

                              ILAN

All the time.

                              MIA

They do. I mean, sometimes.

                              TESS

When?

                              MIA

(looks in mirror) Usually after it's too late.

SCENE 4

> *NICK suddenly bursts into the girls bathroom.*

                              NICK

Makayla?!

                              ILAN

(overlapping TESS and MIA) Oh my GAH! Are you lost?!

                              TESS

(overlapping ILAN and MIA) What are you doing in here?!

                              MIA

(overlapping ILAN and TESS) Nick! Get out! Right now!

                              NICK

Is Makayla in here?

ILAN
Does it look like Makayla is in here?

NICK
One of the stalls?

TESS
Why don't you look?

>*NICK opens every stall without regard to who might be in there.*

MIA
(measured, appalled) Oh my gah I cannot believe you are just looking in the stalls like there might be somebody in there.

ILAN
What if there is somebody in there?

TESS
All this time we've been talking?

NICK
(grabs ILAN by the shoulders) I gotta find Makayla.

ILAN
Guess where she's not? *(beat)* Exactly.

>*SOPHIA and SAGE enter.*

SAGE
(overlapping SOPHIA) Oh my gah, Nick! What are you doing in here?!

SOPHIA
(overlapping SAGE) Nick! What in the world –

NICK

Looking for Makayla, okay? I'm looking for Makayla!

TESS

I'm getting out of here.

MIA

Me, too.

ILAN

Bye. So weird.

TESS, MIA and ILAN hurry out.

NICK

Where is she?

SOPHIA

Not here.

NICK

You sure?

SAGE

You just opened every stall in the building.

NICK

She's not answering her phone.

SOPHIA

That might be on purpose.

NICK

Yeah, well, I need to talk to her.

SAGE

About what?

                              NICK
About what do you think?

                              SOPHIA
If you mean the picture –

                              NICK
I didn't take it.

                              SAGE
Nobody said you did.

                              NICK
Everybody's saying I did!

                              SOPHIA
Everybody says everything in this school.

          Bell rings.

                              NICK
I walked out of that room for like two minutes.

                              SAGE
Which room?

                              NICK
You know which room.

                              SOPHIA
Nick –

                              NICK
And when I came back, people were laughing and doing all
that same stuff.

                         SOPHIA
People laugh when they're uncomfortable.

                          NICK
Yeah? Well, someone had their phone out.

                          SAGE
Gimme a break, everybody had their phone out – that's what
everybody does!

                          NICK
Exactly. So why is everybody blaming me?

                         SOPHIA
(beat) What are you going to say to her?

                          NICK
The truth.

                          SAGE
Which is?

                          NICK
That I didn't know someone took a picture.

                         SOPHIA
That's not the whole truth.

                          NICK
What does that mean?

                          SAGE
It means people remember things differently than you do.

                          NICK
I'm not lying!

SOPHIA

No one said you were.

SAGE

But what you remember might not be what she remembers.

HAZELL enters.

HAZELL

Oh. Oh. Sorry. I – sorry.

SAGE

It's okay, don't mind him.

HAZELL goes into a stall, closes door, puts latch on.

SAGE

He's a senior. Thinks he can do whatever he wants.

Bell rings.

SOPHIA

We are in so much trouble if the monitor comes in here.

SAGE

(imitating a monitor) Do you have a hall pass, young man?

NICK

(beat) So what? Everyone just thinks I'm the bad guy now?

SOPHIA

That's not how this works.

NICK

Feels like it.

SAGE

Nick –

                         NICK
I just need to find her.

                        SOPHIA
Why don't you check the girls bathroom on the second
floor?

                         NICK
That's not funny!

                        SOPHIA
What? Of course it's funny! Gah, c'mon.

                         SAGE
Okay, let's say you find her. Then what?

                         NICK
Then she hears it from me.

                         SAGE
Before she hears it from everyone else.

                        SOPHIA
(low) If she hasn't already.

                         NICK
If you see her –

                        SOPHIA
We will.

        Bell rings.

                         NICK
Just – just tell her I'm looking for her.

        He exits quickly.

SCENE 5

SOPHIA

(exhales) Well.

SAGE

That was a disaster.

SOPHIA

That was a preview.

SAGE

And that was the bell.

SOPHIA

I don't care. I have to check my hair. And this stupid bra is pinching my back.

Three long buzzes followed by an announcement:

RECORDED VOICEOVER

Lockdown! Lockdown! Lockdown!

SOPHIA

Oh my gah what're we gonna do?

SAGE

We're not supposed to be in here during a lockdown drill!

SOPHIA

Are you sure this is a drill?

SAGE

What are you talking about? Yes, it's a drill! It was in the announcements!

SOPHIA

What do we do? Do we stay here?

SAGE

If we get caught in the hallway we'll be in so much trouble.

Three long buzzes then:

RECORDED VOICEOVER

Lockdown! Lockdown! Lockdown!

SOPHIA

Are we supposed to go to another classroom?

SAGE

What if they don't let us in?

SOPHIA

Oh my gah what if this isn't a drill?

SAGE

What?!

SOPHIA

What if it's a real incident and it just happens to coincide with the drill?

SAGE

Stop it!

SOPHIA

Stop what?

SAGE

Stop freaking out! You're making me nervous!

HAZELL is crying in the stall.

SOPHIA

Shhh!

SAGE

What?

SOPHIA

Listen!

More crying.

SAGE

Oh my gah that girl –

SOPHIA just looks at SAGE.

SAGE

– who just came in here!

*SAGE and SOPHIA scramble to the stall where
HAZELL is and knock gently.*

SAGE

Hello? Are you in there?

SOPHIA

Hello?

SAGE

Can we come in? I mean, can you come out?

HAZELL
(through stall door, small) I'm here.

SOPHIA

Are you okay?

HAZELL

I don't know.

SAGE

It's just a lockdown drill.

HAZELL

How do you know?

SAGE

Because they said it was.

HAZELL

But they always say that.

SOPHIA

Yeah, but –

Three long buzzes then:

RECORDED VOICEOVER

Lockdown! Lockdown! Lockdown!

SAGE

See? That's the drill voice.

SOPHIA

What does that even mean?

SAGE

It means it's calm.

SOPHIA

A voice can't be calm.

HAZELL

My heart is beating so loud.

114

                           SOPHIA
That happens to me, too.

                            SAGE
You can come out. We're not going anywhere.

          *The stall door unlocks. HAZELL steps out. Her eyes
          are red; she's trying very hard to hold herself
          together.*

                           SOPHIA
Hi.

                            SAGE
We're supposed to turn the lights off.

          SOPHIA dashes for the light switch, turns it off.

          *SOPHIA moves toward being under a sink. SAGE
          goes to her then waves HAZELL to join them.*

          Three long buzzes then:

                    RECORDED VOICEOVER
Lockdown! Lockdown! Lockdown!

                           SOPHIA
Hey, it's okay.

                            SAGE
Yeah. Just breathe.

                           SOPHIA
What's your name?

                           HAZELL
Hazell.

                              SAGE

Hi, Hazell.

                             SOPHIA

I'm Sophia. This is Sage.

                             HAZELL

(nodding, wiping her eyes) Do they do these drills often?

                              SAGE

At least once or twice a year. Are you new here?

                             HAZELL

Yeah. I transferred a month ago.

                             SOPHIA

Oh gah. That must be so hard.

                              SAGE

Everyone hates lockdown drills.

                             HAZELL

No, I mean, I hate that we even need them. *(beat)* What if,
one day, it isn't a drill?

                             SOPHIA

They do them so we'll know what to do.

                             HAZELL

But why do we have to know what to do? Why are our
schools like this? *(beat)* My little brother had his first
lockdown drill last year. He's in second grade. The teacher
told them it was just practice, like a fire drill. Like learning
where the exits are. And I guess adults think that if we
practice it enough, it means they're doing something about
it.

HAZELL (CONT)

Like it makes everyone feel safer. Like they're being proactive. Like they're actually doing something about it.

He asked my mom if someone was coming to hurt them. He's seven. Why does a seven-year-old have to think about that?

SAGE

I don't know.

SOPHIA gently nudges HAZELL'S shoulder.

SOPHIA

Hey. Right now, it's just the three of us.

SAGE

And we're okay.

SOPHIA

Hey. Hazell. Who are your friends here?

HAZELL

I don't have any.

SAGE

Well, that's not entirely true. At least, not anymore.

SOPHIA

Yeah.

SAGE

You've got two right here.

HAZELL

Really?

SOPHIA

Sure.

SAGE

You can call us friends.

HAZELL

(lets out a small breath she didn't know she was holding)
Thank you.

PA SYSTEM clicks on.

PRINCIPAL WALTERS

(voiced by DESANTIS) Attention students and staff. The
lockdown drill has now concluded. The lockdown drill has
now concluded. Thank you for your cooperation and for
following safety procedures. Teachers, please unlock your
doors and resume normal classroom activities. Students,
remain in your classrooms and wait for your teacher's
instructions. Again, the lockdown drill is over. Thank you for
taking the drill seriously. Have a good afternoon.

PA SYSTEM clicks off.

SOPHIA

We are in so much trouble.

SAGE

Did you come here with a hall pass?

HAZELL

(shows her hall pass) Yeah.

SOPHIA

Well, you're off the hook.

SAGE

We? Are dead.

SCENE 6

MAKAYLA bursts in, turns on the light switch.

MAKAYLA

What are you all doing in here?

SOPHIA

What're we doing in here? What're you doing in here?

MAKAYLA

(holds up her hall pass) I have a hall pass!

HAZELL

(shows her hall pass) Me, too.

SOPHIA

(to MAKAYLA) Who cares about a stupid hall pass? We were
caught in here during that lockdown drill!

MAKAYLA

Oh – what did you do?

SAGE

We just sat here.

MAKAYLA

With the light off?

SOPHIA

It's what we're supposed to do, Makayla!

HAZELL

I have a hall pass, too.

MAKAYLA

(not really listening but still to HAZELL) That's awesome.
Who are you?

HAZELL

Hazell.

SAGE

She's our friend.

MAKAYLA

(not entirely sincere) Again, awesome.

SAGE

What are you doing here? I thought your mom was picking
you up.

MAKAYLA

She was, then Ms. DeSantis talked me down; then the
lockdown drill happened, so I called my mom back and told
her to forget it.

SOPHIA

Weren't the three of us in here just a minute ago?

MAKAYLA

Yeah. Feels like a week ago.

SAGE

A lot happened in about an hour.

MAKAYLA

(beat) So. Hazell, right?

HAZELL nods.

MAKAYLA

You picked a very weird day to make friends.

SOPHIA

She didn't pick it. It just sort of… happened.

MAKAYLA

Yeah. That seems to be the theme today.

SAGE

But hey, Makayla, are you okay?

MAKAYLA

(shrugs) Define okay.

SOPHIA

Mak –

MAKAYLA

No, seriously. Like 'okay' okay? Or school 'okay'?

SAGE

Either.

MAKAYLA

Let's go with… still standing.

HAZELL

(sincere) That counts.

MAKAYLA

Yeah. *(softly)* I guess it does.

SOPHIA

So, where were you during physics?

                    MAKAYLA
Guidance.

                    SAGE
Like, the whole time?

                    MAKAYLA
Pretty much.

                    SOPHIA
Including lockdown?

                    MAKAYLA
Yep.

                    SAGE
That must've been fun.

                    MAKAYLA
It was something. Ms. DeSantis made me sit in that chair
that's way too soft.

                    SOPHIA
The blue one.

                    SAGE
That chair makes everything feel serious.

                    MAKAYLA
Exactly. And she just kept handing me tissues like we were
preparing for a hurricane.

                    SOPHIA
You were crying?

                    MAKAYLA
Oh, yeah.

                         SAGE
Same.

                       MAKAYLA
Like, ugly crying.

                        SOPHIA
That tracks.

                       MAKAYLA
At one point I couldn't even talk anymore and she just sat
there.

                         SAGE
Doing the counselor thing.

                       MAKAYLA
Yeah. Just… waiting. It was weird.

                        SOPHIA
How?

                       MAKAYLA
Because she didn't try to fix it.

                         SAGE
That's literally her job.

                       MAKAYLA
No, I mean she didn't say anything like, 'everything will be
fine.'

                        SOPHIA
Because it might not be.

                       MAKAYLA
Right. *(beat)* She said something else.

                         SAGE

What?

                       MAKAYLA

She said sometimes when something bad happens, the
hardest part is realizing you can't control what everyone else
does with it. She said people will talk. People will guess.
People will build whole stories out of one little piece of
something.

                         SAGE

Sounds about right.

                       MAKAYLA

And then she said the only thing I actually get to control is
what I do next.

        HAZELL shifts slightly closer to them.

                       MAKAYLA

She also made me drink water.

                        SOPHIA

Classic DeSantis.

                        HAZELL

My dad does that, too.

                         SAGE

Hydration is healing.

                       MAKAYLA

She literally said that. And when the lockdown started she
was like, 'Well, now you get the full high school experience.'

                         SAGE

Wow.

124

MAKAYLA

We turned off the lights and sat on the floor. Just sat there in the dark.

SOPHIA

That's kind of terrifying.

MAKAYLA

It was weirdly calm.

SAGE

Because you were already having the worst day imaginable.

MAKAYLA

Pretty much.

HAZELL

Sometimes, quiet helps.

MAKAYLA

(beat) Yeah. It does. What's your name again?

HAZELL

Hazell.

MAKAYLA

Hazell. Got it.

SAGE

So.

SOPHIA

So.

SAGE

What happens now?

MAKAYLA

Apparently, I go back to class.

SOPHIA

Like a normal day.

MAKAYLA

Like a normal day. *(beat)* Well, after I go to the bathroom first. *(goes to stall)*

HAZELL

I have a hall pass.

MAKAYLA

(opening stall door) What?

HAZELL

(shows her hall pass) I have a hall pass.

MAKAYLA

Oh, that's right. You do *(goes into stall, closes door)*.

SAGE

(to HAZELL) Don't mind her. She's having a day.

MAKAYLA

(from inside stall) I heard that!

SAGE

See what I mean?

MAKAYLA

(still inside stall) I heard that, too!

SCENE 7

ALEX and EMERSON burst the door open.

SAGE

Oh my gah!

SOPHIA

What are you two doing?!

ALEX AND EMERSON

We're looking for Nick!

EMERSON

Nick, we're looking for Nick.

SOPHIA

Emerson? In the girls' bathroom?

ALEX

We looked everywhere else.

SAGE

And the girls' bathroom isn't off-limits or anything, right?

EMERSON

What are you talking about? I've got a hall pass.

SAGE

What?

EMERSON

Well, I did have one.

SOPHIA

Not to go to the girls' bathroom!

BRENNA, TESS, and ILAN enter.

BRENNA

(mid-story) …and that's when I told him, *(sees boys)* oh my gah!

ILAN

What is going on in here?!

ALEX

Nothing! We're just trying to find Nick!

> *HAZELL moves to the far edge of the sinks, away from the action.*

EMERSON

(referring to HAZELL) Who is that?

SAGE

None of your business!

SOPHIA

She's a girl, she's allowed in here!

TESS

Unlike you guys!

EMERSON

Never mind, let's go Alex.

ILAN

Wait, wait! *(everyone freezes)* Nick was in here earlier.

ALEX

I knew it!

EMERSON

What was Nick doing in here?

ILAN

Looking for Makayla.

SOPHIA

Oh, Makayla is –

SAGE

(quickly) Not here!

SOPHIA

Sage?

SAGE

(nervously) Because she, she had that double period and the exam – and then she went to guidance and she was there during the whole lockdown drill.

EMERSON

Everybody's looking for Makayla – or more like, looking at Makayla.

SOPHIA

Shut up!

SAGE

It's not funny!

EMERSON

What? Gimme a break! I don't care what she does!

SAGE

Yeah? Well, I can guarantee you that she does!

SOPHIA

Why don't you guys just get out of here!

ALEX

We will! Sorry! Okay? Come on, Emerson, let's go.

EMERSON

(turns to go, then turns back) You know, we didn't come in here to be jerks. We just wanted to find our friend.

SCENE 8

NICK bursts in, almost knocking ALEX over.

ALEX

Whoa, whoa! Nick! Dude! Where've you been?

NICK

What're you guys doing in here?

BRENNA

Exactly what we've been trying to figure out.

EMERSON

We told you! We're looking for Nick!

TESS

News flash – he's right there.

NICK

Okay, okay – everybody relax.

ALEX

Relax? Dude, the whole school is losing its mind.

ILAN

Why?

ALEX

Because of – *(EMERSON elbows him)* because people are bored!

SAGE

That's the worst lie I've ever heard.

SOPHIA

Seriously.

NICK

Can everyone just stop talking for a second?

BRENNA

You're in the girls' bathroom! Talking is what we do!

TESS

And you three are guys!

ILAN

This is a violation of at least four school policies!

TESS

Five!

BRENNA

Six!

EMERSON

Oh, please.

SAGE

You burst in here like it's Grand Central Station!

ALEX

We said we're sorry!

                              TESS

This is chaos!

                              ILAN

This is exactly why drills exist!

                            EMERSON

What does that even mean?

                              ILAN

It means people panic and run into rooms they're not
supposed to be in!

                              ALEX

We didn't panic!

                            EMERSON

We navigated strategically.

                              SAGE

You navigated into the girls' bathroom.

                             BRENNA

Which is illegal!

                              TESS

It's not illegal!

                             BRENNA

It should be!

                              NICK

Can SOMEONE! Just tell me. If Makayla. Is okay?

          *SAGE turns her head ever so slightly toward the
          stalls to see if MAKAYLA wants to make an
          appearance. Nothing. SAGE gives a slight shrug.*

SOPHIA

Why wouldn't she be?

EMERSON

Because everyone's talking about it.

SCENE 9

FIONA, GABRIELA, and MIA enter.

GABRIELA

What in the name of town hall gatherings is going on in here?!

TESS

Oh my gah, Gabby, we don't have time to explain it all.

ILAN

There are, like, twelve people in a room designed for four. Statistically, this is a terrible idea.

BRENNA

If you have to pee, go pee. Otherwise, stand back and listen.

NICK

Listen? This isn't for everybody!

FIONA

Apparently it is!

ALEX

Forget it, man, she's not here.

EMERSON

And we're just talking in the girls' bathroom like it's the courtyard.

                          SAGE
No, wait! I want to know what everyone's talking about.

                        EMERSON
You know exactly what!

                          MIA
I hate this.

                          ILAN
Same.

                          ALEX
Look, bro, we should go.

                          NICK
(beat) I just need to talk to her.

                        MAKAYLA
(from inside stall) Unbelievable.

                          NICK
Who said that?

                        SOPHIA
(coughs, then) Okay, everybody out!

                          SAGE
Yes! Bathroom closed!

                        BRENNA
Girls only!

                          FIONA
Evacuate!

GABRIELA

(points to door) This is a restricted facility!

ALEX

We're leaving!

EMERSON

Relax.

HAZELL

(still somewhat apart from the others, loudly at first)
Maybe… *(everyone slowly turns toward HAZELL)* everyone
should just pause.

SOPHIA

Pause? We've been pausing all day!

SAGE

No, we've been reacting all day.

EMERSON

What is that supposed to mean?

BRENNA

It means people are staring and whispering and pretending
they're not.

ALEX

Happens every day in this school.

ILAN

Not like this.

FIONA

Exactly.

EMERSON
Okay, but why is everyone acting like the guys did something?

SAGE
Because guys usually do.

ALEX
That is so unfair.

GABRIELA
Is it?

TESS
Look at the dress code.

EMERSON
What about it?

TESS
Girls get sent home for showing their shoulders.

ILAN
Or for wearing shorts that are "too short."

BRENNA
Or leggings.

FIONA
Or tank tops.

SOPHIA
Or literally existing in a female body.

MIA
Anything that might cause a 'distraction' to boys.

                              ALEX

Guys have rules, too.

                              SAGE

Name one.

                              ALEX

(beat) Hats.

                              TESS

Oh, wow. Hats.

                              ILAN

The injustice.

                              ALEX

I'm serious!

                           BRENNA
Girls get clothes measured with rulers!

                          GABRIELA
(imitating a monitor) 'Pull that down – don't want to cause a
distraction for the boys.'

                           FIONA
Girls get told to sit a certain way.

                           TESS
Girls get told to smile more.

                           FIONA
(contemptuously) It improves their face-value.

                           MIA
Girls get told to calm down.

                              ALEX

Okay, okay –

                            EMERSON

But that's not on us!

                              SAGE

It kinda is.

                            EMERSON

How?

                              SAGE

Because nobody ever tells boys they're distracting.

                              ALEX

Well, that's because – *(stops himself)*

                            BRENNA

Exactly.

                              ILAN

Girls have to get up at least an hour earlier than guys to get
ready for school.

                              NICK

I don't get it.

                            SOPHIA

What don't you get, Mister Lacrosse Captain?

                              NICK

The whole thing about girls dressing up for guys.

                              SAGE

That's because you're not paying attention.

NICK

No, I am paying attention. *(beat)* Here's what I don't get. I don't get why girls wear makeup at all. I mean, I don't care if girls wear makeup or not. I actually think makeup is ridiculous.

SOPHIA

Gimme a break.

NICK

No, I'm serious! I don't care. I think girls can be beautiful just the way they are. I mean, I'm not after every single girl, I'm just saying that there's no reason to put on all that makeup and stuff.

SOPHIA

Oh, c'mon, Nick. You know you want girls to wear makeup.

NICK

No! No I don't! And I'll tell you something else. Girls don't put on makeup for guys. Because none of us care! We don't! Emerson, do you care if girls wear makeup?

EMERSON

No.

NICK

Alex, you?

ALEX

I kinda wish they wouldn't. Especially my sister who takes up the bathroom for hours putting it on.

NICK

See?

SOPHIA

All right, Nick. If girls don't put makeup on for guys, who do they put it on for? Themselves?

NICK

Other girls! I'm serious! Other girls. *(beat)* Think about it. Girls get all done up for other girls. You all act like there's a double-standard about stuff but girls do just as much as boys do to create that problem.

GABRIELA

Oh, come on, we do not!

NICK

Look, if girls think we're sitting there looking and judging every little thing they do, they're wrong!

MIA

Oh, yeah?

NICK

Yeah!

EMERSON

Most of the time, we're just trying not to look stupid.

FIONA

He's got a point. Girls are smarter than boys.

ALEX

Oh, come on! We're not gonna fight about that, are we?

NICK

Well, she's not wrong. Girls do better than boys in just about every subject including math and science.

ILAN

I know I do.

NICK

I know you do! You're in my trig class and you're a junior.
What's your average?

ILAN

93.

NICK

I can't beat that. I could never beat that!

TESS

So, if girls are smarter than boys, what happens in college?

SAGE

What happens is girls go to college and major in things like
Communication, Fashion, Teacher, Social Work…

SOPHIA

While guys major in things that matter…

BRENNA

And make real money.

MIA

Because that's what boys do and girls just… don't.

EMERSON

What? Who tells you that?

FIONA

Everybody! Mom, dad, grandparents.

BRENNA

Guidance counselors.

                              ILAN
Teachers.

                            GABRIELA
Movies.

                              MIA
Social media.

                             SAGE
Basically the entire planet.

                           EMERSON
That's ridiculous!

                             ALEX
Yeah, nobody's forcing you to major in anything.

                            SOPHIA
No one forces you either, but somehow you all end up
running everything.

                             TESS
That escalated.

                             NICK
Okay. Can we not turn this into a sociology lecture?

                             SAGE
You started it!

                             NICK
I didn't start it!

                            BRENNA
You literally said makeup was ridiculous!

                           NICK

Because it is!

                          SOPHIA

Easy for you to say! You roll out of bed and look exactly the
same.

                           ALEX

That is not true.

                         GABRIELA

It absolutely is!

                           ILAN

You people put on a hoodie and call it an outfit.

                         EMERSON

That hoodie is a lifestyle.

                           MIA

This is exhausting.

                           SAGE

Okay! This has gone far enough.

                           NICK

What does that mean?

                           SAGE

It means everyone's standing here – in the girls' bathroom –

                          FIONA

Emphasis on girls!

                           SAGE

- arguing about philosophy while the actual person
  everyone's talking about –

                         NICK

What?

                        SOPHIA

Sage.

                         SAGE

No. I'm serious.

SCENE 10

> *The stall door slowly opens. MAKAYLA steps out.*

> *The room goes silent.*

                       MAKAYLA

Wow. You all managed to turn my entire life into a panel
discussion.

> *NICK takes a step forward.*

                         NICK

Makayla –

                       MAKAYLA

Don't. Just… don't start with my name like that.

                         TESS

(whispering to BRENNA) This is worse than lockdown.

                        BRENNA

Way worse.

                       MAKAYLA

How many people are in here?

                       GABRIELA

(counts, then) Too many.

MAKAYLA

Yeah. That sounds about right. *(beat)* So. Which one of you wants to tell me what story everyone's telling now?

NICK

Makayla, maybe everyone should just… *(gestures to the door)* give us a minute.

MAKAYLA

No.

NICK

What?

MAKAYLA

No. Since everyone apparently knows about the picture, I think everyone should hear what happened. And whatever you have to say. I mean, does anyone here not know about the picture? *(beat, nothing)* Okay, if you don't know, raise your hand.

> *HAZELL slowly raises her hand. Everyone looks at her.*

MAKAYLA

You don't know?

HAZELL

No.

MAKAYLA

Okay. Whoever you are, you can go.

SAGE

(to MAKAYLA and HAZELL) No! No. Stay. *(to MAKAYLA)* Her name is Hazell. She's our friend. She's a good person.

MAKAYLA

Okay. Well, maybe this will actually make sense to at least
one person in the room.

NICK

Makayla, you don't have to –

MAKAYLA

I kind of do. Because everyone else already decided what it
means. *(beat)* There was a party.

EMERSON

We know.

MAKAYLA

(referring to HAZELL) She doesn't! There was a party. At
the Westbrook girls' house.

BRENNA

The twins.

ILAN

They're not twins.

GABRIELA

They dress like twins.

MAKAYLA

There were like, fifty people there. Maybe more. Phones
were everywhere. You couldn't walk three steps without
someone filming something.

NICK

That's just every party now.

146

MAKAYLA

Exactly. So, here's my question. How many people in this
room have a phone?

Bell rings.

MAKAYLA

Nobody goes anywhere!

TESS

We'll be late!

MAKAYLA

I don't care. How many people in this room have a phone?

ALL raise their hand.

MAKAYLA

Everyone. Right. How many people in this room saw the
picture?

ALL hands go up slowly.

MAKAYLA

Okay. How many people forwarded it?

Beat. Then BRENNA raises her hand slightly.

BRENNA

I did. *(beat)* I'm sorry.

MAKAYLA

Thank you for saying that.

ILAN raises her hand.

                    ILAN
I sent it to one person. I didn't think it would go anywhere.
You don't even think about it. It's just tap… send… done.
And –

                    MIA
I opened it. *(beat)* I didn't send it.

                    TESS
I almost did.

                    EMERSON
I saw it.

                    ALEX
Same.

          SAGE and SOPHIA exchange a glance.

              SOPHIA and SAGE
We saw it.

                    SOPHIA
You know we saw it.

                    SAGE
But we didn't send it.

                    MAKAYLA
Okay. So that's what, ten people?

                    BRENNA
Something like that.

                    MAKAYLA
Ten people in this bathroom. Now imagine the whole school.

148

NICK

Makayla, I swear I didn't –

MAKAYLA

Take the picture?

> *NICK stops.*

MAKAYLA

I know.

EMERSON

Wait. You do?

MAKAYLA

Yeah. Because when it happened… *(stops, considers)*. Or,
when it must have happened… Here's the thing. I don't
know who took it either. There were too many phones. Too
many people. Too much noise. One second everyone's
laughing, having a good time, and the next second… there's
a picture.

NICK

I left the room for like two minutes.

MAKAYLA

And when you came back, people were already looking at
their screens.

NICK

Exactly.

SAGE

So literally anyone could've taken it.

ILAN

Anyone with a phone.

BRENNA

Which is everyone.

HAZELL

So, everyone helped make the story.

MAKAYLA

What?

HAZELL

Everyone helped make the story. Even if they didn't mean to.

ALEX

Why are you talking? You weren't even there.

SAGE

It doesn't matter, Alex! Let her talk! Gah.

SCENE 11

HAZELL

(beat) I think… we're all a little confused about what we're actually looking at.

A few minutes ago, everyone in here was arguing about makeup and dress codes and distractions. About how girls are told what to do and what not to do so they don't cause problems for someone else.

> *DESANTIS quietly enters the bathroom. She stands in the back, unnoticed.*

And then he *(referring to NICK)* said something. He said girls don't wear makeup for guys. They wear it for other girls. *(Beat)* Maybe that's true. Or maybe it's not about who we're doing it for.

HAZELL (CONT)

Maybe it's just that all of us are trying to put on something
that helps us get through the day. Like a mask. Not a fake
mask. Just… something that makes the world easier to walk
through.

We all want people to see the version of us that feels… safer.

But pictures don't see that. Pictures freeze one moment. One
tiny second. And suddenly that second becomes the whole
story.

But nobody is just one second.

And if we don't decide who we are for ourselves, other
people will do it for us. And that's when a picture turns into
a story. And a story turns into judgment. And suddenly
someone else is writing your life.

MAKAYLA

That was… a lot. But you're not wrong.

HAZELL

Sorry.

MAKAYLA

No. Don't apologize. *(looks around the room, doesn't see
DESANTIS)* Okay. So here's the part everyone thinks they
understand. Nick and I were talking. Just talking. We were in
a room. Maybe I fell asleep… And somebody took a picture.
That's it.

BRENNA

That's… not what people are saying.

MAKAYLA

I know.

151

SAGE

People filled in the rest.

MAKAYLA

Exactly.

NICK

Makayla –

MAKAYLA

No. You don't have to defend me.

NICK

I wasn't –

MAKAYLA

I know you weren't.

EMERSON

So… if nobody knows who took it –

ILAN

Then why is everyone acting like they do?

TESS

Because a mystery is uncomfortable.

MIA

So people make something up.

SAGE

I'm sorry for all this, Kay.

BRENNA

Me, too.

SOPHIA

That's kinda what we do as humans.

> *Silence. Then a calm voice from the back of the room.*

DESANTIS

Yes. *(steps forward)* It is.

ALEX

Oh my –

FIONA

How long have you been standing there?

DESANTIS

Long enough. That was one of the more thoughtful conversations I've overheard in the girls' bathroom.

GABRIELA

Oh my gah. Did you hear everything?

DESANTIS

I heard honesty. Which, I should point out, is a rare thing in high school hallways. And sometimes even rarer in adult ones. What I heard was a room full of people trying to understand something that happened very quickly.

A picture. A story that grew faster than the truth. That happens more often than you think.

But something else happened here. You talked to each other. You listened. You even apologized. That matters.

However. This is still a school. And this is still the girls' bathroom. And there's a number of you that don't belong in

153

DESANTIS (CONT)
here. So. Everyone except Nick and Makayla – please go
back to class. *(beat)* That wasn't a suggestion.

TESS
We're between bells. We need a hall pass.

DESANTIS
Forget the hall passes. I'll talk to your teachers. Just go.

*Everyone begins to file out of the bathroom.
HAZELL is last.*

HAZELL
You're more than one second.

MAKAYLA
Wait!

HAZELL turns back toward MAKAYLA.

MAKAYLA
Hazell, right?

HAZELL nods.

MAKAYLA rushes to HAZELL, hugs her.

MAKAYLA
I love you, girl.

They part. HAZELL exits.

DESANTIS
You two seem to have the rest of the conversation. I
recommend you have it honestly. *(goes to the door)* And for
the record, high school stories have a short shelf-life. Truth
tends to outlast them *(exits quietly)*.

SCENE 12

                         NICK
So.

                       MAKAYLA
So.

                         NICK
I didn't take the picture.

                       MAKAYLA
I know.

                         NICK
Okay. Do you hate me?

                       MAKAYLA
No. But I do hate how fast everyone decided what it meant.

                         NICK
Yeah.

                       MAKAYLA
Including you.

                         NICK
(beat) That's fair.

> *MAKAYLA looks toward the mirrors over the sinks —
> where they would be positioned. She studies her
> reflection.*

                       MAKAYLA
You know the weird part?

                    NICK

What?

                  MAKAYLA

That picture doesn't even look like me.

       NICK steps beside her, also facing the mirror.

                    NICK

That's because it's not the whole picture.

              MAKAYLA looks at him.

                  MAKAYLA

Exactly.

                    NICK

You okay?

                  MAKAYLA

I will be. Eventually.

                    NICK

Okay. *(checking his face in mirror)* That was the wildest day
in my life.

                  MAKAYLA

You're the captain of the lacrosse team. I'm pretty sure
you've had wilder days.

                    NICK

Nope. This is number one.

                  MAKAYLA

Really?

NICK

(still looking in mirror) We had a lockdown drill, a sociology debate, and a full town hall meeting in the girls' bathroom.

MAKAYLA

What, you need a little powder or something? Some lip gloss?

NICK

Stop it.

MAKAYLA

Come on, let's turn the tables – you put on makeup for girls.

NICK

Never happen.

MAKAYLA

(teasing) Oh, wait! Better idea: you put on makeup for guys!

NICK

(teasing) For guys? I'm leaving.

MAKAYLA

(more teasing) No, no! Come on! Make a name for yourself! The lacrosse captain who wears makeup!

NICK

I don't think I need anything else to go with my name.

They laugh.

MAKAYLA

I didn't really need anything else to go with my name, either. And after today, everybody knows my name.

NICK

Pretty sure they already did. You're 'Makayla.'

MAKAYLA

Not like this.

NICK

Yeah. Sorry. About all of it.

MAKAYLA

It's not your fault.

NICK

That's the nicest thing anyone's said to me all day.

MAKAYLA

Don't get used to it.

NICK

What? *(beat)* Okay.

MAKAYLA

Okay.

NICK

Um. This might be the worst possible time to ask this question.

MAKAYLA

That sounds promising.

NICK

The Winter Dance is coming up.

MAKAYLA

Yes. I'm aware.

NICK

And before today happened, I was gonna ask if you – if you weren't already going with someone –

MAKAYLA

Nick.

NICK

Yeah?

MAKAYLA

You're asking me to the Winter Dance? Today? In the girls' bathroom?

NICK

Technically, I'm asking you after the Bathroom Summit of [*current year*].

MAKAYLA

The bathroom summit.

NICK

Historic moment.

MAKAYLA

Truly.

NICK

Pretty much reset the entire day.

MAKAYLA

Oh, did it?

NICK

(beat) So, what do you think?

MAKAYLA

I think… you have incredibly bad timing.

NICK

I've been told that.

MAKAYLA

But at least you asked in person.

NICK

Seemed safer than texting.

MAKAYLA gives a soft laugh.

MAKAYLA

The Winter Dance, huh? *(beat)* Okay. I'll go with you.

NICK

No way! Really?

MAKAYLA

Really.

NICK

Really??

MAKAYLA

Really.

NICK

Yes! Score! *(realizes what he said)* No, no, Makayla! I didn't mean it like that! Seriously! I mean –

MAKAYLA

Nick?

NICK

Yeah?

MAKAYLA

(she has the power) Get out of here.

NICK

Oh. Yeah. Okay. Talk to you later *(exits)*.

> *MAKAYLA looks in the mirror. Checks her makeup, hair, clothes.*

MAKAYLA

Oh, Makayla, Makayla.

> *After a moment, her phone rings, she smiles when she looks at the caller. Her delivery is gentle, not rushed.*

Hi mom.
I'm good.

Better.
Yeah. Yeah, I remember.

"This, too, shall pass."

I know.
I know.
Yeah.
I'm okay.
Thanks.

I love you, too.
Bye.

> *She puts her phone away. She looks at herself in the mirror. Takes a deep breath.*

MAKAYLA (CONT)

This, too, shall pass.

Lights fade down as music fades up.

End of Play